C000243214

RAILWAYS IN AND ARC

NEWTON ABBOT

AND

TORBAY

Newton Abbot, 18th July 1956. The Down 'Cornish Riviera' passes Newton Abbot racecourse and heads towards the station. With a load of only nine coaches and West Box distant signal 'off', it does not appear that 'King' class 4-6-0 No.**6024** *King Edward I* will be stopping for an assistant engine, although the timetable made provision for it. This Locomotive was one of several of the class based at Laira (Plymouth) and has since been restored by the Quainton Railway Centre, Aylesbury.

R.C. Riley

C. R. POTTS

Copyright © 1993 Foxline Publishing and C.R. Potts
ISBN 1 870119 25 8
All rights reserved
Designed and Edited by Gregory K. Fox
Typeset by Bill Rear, Johnstown, Wrexham
Printed by the Amadeus Press, Huddersfield

Published by Foxline Publishing
32, Urwick Road, Romiley, Stockport. SK6 3JS

By the same author:
The Brixham Branch (pub. Oakwood Press)
The Newton Abbot to Kingswear Railway 1844-1988 (pub. Oakwood Press)

Contents ...

(left). **Newton Abbot. c.1927.**
Tobacco kiosk. *British Rail.*

Introduction

Although Newton Abbot was at the hub of a wheel spreading to Moretonhampstead in the north, towards Exeter in the east, to Kingswear in the south and to Totnes and Ashburton in the west, all of these other lines have had books written about them. Newton Abbot itself has not, so I have slanted the photographic content in Newton Abbot's favour, but still ensured that the other photogenic lines mentioned have received ample attention.

It is heartening that only one of the lines described in this book has closed completely - the 2 miles-long Brixham branch. Two others were scheduled for closure, the section from Paignton to Kingswear and the Ashburton branch. The former did not close but was taken over by the Dart Valley Railway in 1972 without a break, whilst the latter branch closed in 1962, reopened after a period of seven years, again in private ownership, although forced to terminate at Buckfastleigh, some two years later, by the Government's road-building needs. The Moretonhampstead branch lost its passenger service early, but remains open for freight for some $1/3$ of its length. The main line of course is one of InterCity's trunk routes and although much rationalised from the scenes in this book is still able to be used as the most pleasant and relaxing way to admire Devon's sea and country scenery.

Readers will find the names of some well-respected photographers of the West Country railway scene within these pages, indeed it has been a pleasure choosing from their photographs and writing the captions, and I thank them all for the excellence of their material. I particularly wish to thank David Fish for letting me choose photographs, despite his own publishing requirements, and for finding time in his busy farming schedule to print them for me. And, having been an avid follower of Peter Gray's weekly 'Rail Trail' column in the *Torquay Herald Express* for many years, it gives me great pleasure to reproduce a good number of his photographs. Peter also found time to read the manuscript, correct my mistakes and supply additional background information. I am very grateful to him. Derek Frost furnished me with some missing dates and engine numbers, which the reader will appreciate. Peter Kay extracted entries from a log book dating back to 1901 kept by the Newton Abbot station masters; some of the details feature in the 'Newton Abbot chronology' herein.

Having known Newton Abbot through some of its 'busy' years, it is so sad to see it now, just a medium sized calling place standing in acres of waste ground formerly occupied by locomotive works, engine shed and sidings. Hackney Yard is no more, nor is the goods shed or the signal boxes along with most of the staff! One can hardly imagine, now, the Great Western's massive investment in the town over several decades. I hope therefore that these pages will remind the older reader of how things once were, and help make the younger reader, who might sit on the empty station gazing over the weeds and rubble, aware of the business of the place and the importance it once played in the life of both the town and the West Country. *Sic transit gloria mundi.*

Christopher Potts
Didcot.

Newton Abbot. 21st March 1951. Awaiting departure time with the 0.40am stopping train for Exeter is Newton Abbot (83A) based 2-6-2T No.**4109**. This service was advertised as Third Class only, took three quarters of an hour for the twenty mile journey. *R.J. Buckley.*

Parson's Tunnel to Newton Abbot

Many people regard the section along the sea wall between Dawlish and Teignmouth as the most attractive part of the former GWR. Some would disagree with the word 'most' and put another location in top place (for attractiveness), but would probably agree that it is the most memorable part of the system.

In the days when railways moved the great bulk of the population from their place of work to their holiday destination for the brief one or two weeks respite they had long looked forward to, the line between Starcross and Teignmouth gave them their first glimpse of the sea. Despite serving seaside resorts throughout Devon and Cornwall, the GWR's main line did not come close to the coast very often and this section had to be savoured. On summer Saturdays, of course, progress was often very slow and there was plenty of

opportunity to watch people enjoying themselves on Dawlish and Teignmouth beaches. On a good day when traffic was moving (and certainly nowadays), the time spent beside the sea was tantalisingly short, and unless you were travelling to Torbay it was quite some time before you saw the sea again.

This book starts with a train leaving Parson's Tunnel and thus readers can enjoy a short section of the sea wall before Teignmouth is reached and the trains in our pictures turn inland and run alongside the River Teign, which is very attractive in a completely different way, before passing Hackney Yard (on the left) and the green expanse of Newton Abbot Racecourse (on the right) and arriving at one of the West Country's principal junction stations, Newton Abbot.

Parson's Tunnel, October 1956. One of Newton Abbot's top locomotives, 'Castle' class 4-6-0 No.**5059** *Earl St. Aldwyn* bursts out of Parson's Tunnel with a Down 'stopper'. Undoubtedly one of David Fish's classic photographs, and observe how clean are the locomotive and carriages in those days before the advent of carriage washing machines in any numbers Generally, the line gradient is now on the descent towards Teignmouth although the curvature of the route limited trains to fairly modest speeds
David S. Fish

Sprey Point. c.1910. A short Down express train heads towards Teignmouth, past Parson's Tunnel signal box and its disused signals. Between 1884 and 1905 the signal box controlled the junction between the double line from Teignmouth and the single line (through Parson's Tunnel and four others) to Dawlish. When the tunnels were widened a double line to Dawlish opened on 1st October 1905, Parson's Tunnel box effectively became redundant and it was closed in 1909, despite the provision of a new structure west of the 1884 box in 1906. This picture would seem to date c.1910, before the signals were removed. The box had a second life, reopened on 2nd July 1934 and closing for the second, and last time, on 1st April 1964.   *Author's collection.*

(Centre). **Sprey Point, 2nd July 1957.** '2884' class 2-8-0 No.**3806**, a Newport Ebbw Jn. locomotive, passes Sprey Point with a Down class 'H' goods. The southern portal to Parson's Tunnel can be seen in the distance by the end of the sea wall.   *R.C. Riley*

Sprey Point, 17th July 1958. A pair of 'Hall' class locomotives double-head the 7.30 am Penzance - Manchester train along the sea wall. No.**4930** *Hagley Hall* is pilot, and No.**6907** *Davenham Hall* the train engine. The photographer has recorded the time as 11.39am and the train is exactly on time, although Mancunians making the northbound journey face another eight hours of travel with an interminable number of stops. A twelve hour journey of 1958 can these days be achieved in around eight albeit with changes. There was however a Refreshment car facility from Plymouth onwards.   *R.C. Riley*

Sprey Point, 1st July 1957. A stranger in the camp! Ex-LMS class '8F' 2-8-0 No.**48475**, based at Bristol (St. Philip's Marsh) passes Parson's Tunnel Up distant signal with a class 'E' goods. The random stonework to the right of the engine highlights one of numerous locations along this section where cliff strengthening was carried out between the wars. *R.C. Riley*

Sprey Point, 19th July 1956. 'Hall' class 4-6-0 No.**4936** *Kinlet Hall* passes Sprey Point approaching Teignmouth with a class 'H' Down goods. *R.C. Riley*

Teignmouth, 19th July 1956. The 11.00am Paignton to York, seen here behind 'Castle' class 4-6-0 No.**5078** *Beaufort*, carried 'A' headlamps but called at all stations between Newton Abbot and Starcross in the 1956 timetable. However, after calling at Exeter (St. David's) it then ran fast to Bristol. Here it is seen leaving Teignmouth. *R.C. Riley.*

Teignmouth - Eastcliff, 18th July 1956. The last 'Star' to survive, No.**4056** *Princess Margaret* is here seen rounding the curve just east of Teignmouth Station with an Up van train from Plymouth. She was withdrawn in October 1957 after spending her last few years at Bristol Bath Road. *R.C. Riley*

Teignmouth - Eastcliff, c 1880. An early view of the approach to Teignmouth before the east end tunnel was opened out and the line through Teignmouth doubled in 1884. There is a disc and crossbar signal just outside the tunnel mouth.

Peter W. Gray Collection

Teignmouth - Eastcliff, 1st July 1957. Laira (Plymouth) based 'Castle' class 4-6-0 No. 7031 *Cromwell's Castle* passes under Eastcliff bridge just east of Teignmouth station with the 7.15 am Plymouth to Paddington express. The driver (or fireman) has obviously decided he wants to be photographed! Leaving Teignmouth at 8.25, a call was made at Dawlish before arriving Exeter at 8.52. The five hour journey to London from Plymouth enjoyed the luxury of a Refreshment Car on which a full breakfast could be obtained for 5/6d (27½p).   *R.C. Riley*

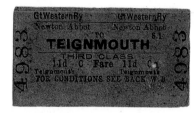

Teignmouth. Teignmouth signal box was situated at the west end of the Down platform. The box closed in November 1986 when colour light signalling, controlled from Exeter, replaced it.
David Nicholas

Teignmouth. 11th July 1956. The 9.30 am Paddington to Newquay train passes Teignmouth Old Quay signal box, hauled by 'Castle' class 4-6-0 No.**7036** *Taunton Castle*. This signal box was only 22 chains west of Teignmouth and was therefore of no value as a break-section box, only being switched in for access to the Old Quay sidings (through the gate, bottom right). *R.C. Riley*

Kingsteignton, Saturday, 15th July 1961. With one too many headcode discs displayed, 'D6300' class diesel No. **D6305** assists 'Castle' class 4-6-0 No.**5042** *Winchester Castle* along the side of the River Teign approaching Newton Abbot. The train is the 12 noon Paddington to Plymouth, a journey which took over 5½ hours, half an hour longer than the Monday-Friday timing.
W.L. Underhay

Teign Estuary. September 1959. Passing freights at the 212¾ m.p. alongside the Teign estuary. The Down train, (further line), is hauled by 'Hall' class 4-6-0 No.**4905** *Barton Hall*.
David S. Fish

Hackney, 13th July 1959. The 10.05 am Exeter to Paignton stopping train hauled by 'Castle' class 4-6-0 No.**5053** *Earl Cairns* passes Hackney 'down home' signal. Calling at all stations apart from Exminster, the train took some 78 minutes for a journey of just over 28 miles. *R.C. Riley*

Hackney, 18th October 1959. BR Standard class '9F' 2-10-0 No.**92223** is pulling well as it heads away from Hackney with a Tavistock Jn - Avonmouth express goods.
David S. Fish

Newton Abbot, 1965. Although a large water tank may be seen in the lower centre of the picture, by the Spring of 1965 when this view was taken, steam's reign at Newton Abbot was over. The north end of the station can be seen extreme right, but this picture was chosen because it shows in the distance the full facilities at a once thriving Hackney yard. Newton Abbot East box can be seen towards the bottom left and Hackney box at the far end of the yard, almost in the dead centre of the picture.

Peter W. Gray

Newton Abbot

From its opening on 30th December 1846, the facilities at Newton Abbot were regularly rendered inadequate by the traffic on offer, the station just having to cope until money became available for expansion. The first station comprised two separate sheds, one for the trains to and from Exeter and Plymouth, and the other for those to and from Torquay (Torre), a line which opened in 1848 and was a short 5 miles dead end branch until extended to Paignton in 1859. By 1859, Newton - it was not called Newton Abbot until 1877 - had expanded to three sheds, but, combined with the single line approaches on either side, was woefully inadequate and the cause of much late running and irregularity in the timetable. The South Devon Railway undertook to rebuild it as a conventional double-sided station at a cost of over £9,000, and the new facilities, including extended locomotive sheds, opened in 1861.

After the closure of the short-lived atmospheric railway operation to Newton Abbot, there had been a locomotive workshop at Newton since 1848 and a carriage repair works since 1849. After the atmospheric debacle the SDR had no money for locomotives of its own, and those made available by the GWR - which at that time only ran on relatively flat terrain - proved unsuitable for the steep Devon banks. The SDR subsequently placed a contract with a Birmingham businessman in 1851 to hire locomotives for a 10 year period, and so twelve 4-4-0 saddle tanks for passenger trains, and four 0-6-0 saddle tanks for goods trains were built specially, being supplied between 1851 and 1855, after which hiring from the GWR ceased. Daniel Gooch's brother W.F. Gooch became the contractor's locomotive superintendent at Newton Abbot.

In 1866 the South Devon Railway took over the working of the locomotives themselves and also bought the engines from the contractor. The latter's locomotive superintendent at Newton, by now John Wright, became the SDR's superintendent. In 1876 the working of the SDR was taken over by the GWR - the companies amalgamated in 1878 - and policy for locomotive matters was taken over by Swindon. G.J. Churchward, who had been a pupil of the SDR locomotive superintendent, transferred to Swindon and worked his way up to become the GWR's locomotive, carriage and wagon superintendent in 1902.

The line south-west of Newton Abbot to Totnes was doubled during the period 1853 to 1855 and the eastern approach from Teignmouth was similarly dealt with in 1865. The Paignton line was extended to Brixham Road (Churston) in 1861 and to Kingswear (for Dartmouth) in 1864. In 1876 the three line section between Newton and Torquay Junction (Aller) was quadrupled, and the first part of the Torquay line, to Kingskerswell, was doubled. At the same time three new signal boxes were built at Newton Abbot with points and signals interlocked.

The next major expansion of facilities at Newton Abbot was associated with the narrowing of the broad gauge between Exeter and Kingswear/Truro in 1892. A sum of £5,000 was authorised for alterations and improvements in the station area and no less than £15,000 for a larger locomotive shed, 100ft x 150ft, opening in 1893.

By the early years of the 20th century, if not sooner, it was apparent that Newton Abbot station was quite inadequate to handle the traffic

Newton Abbot. 13th May 1956 (Sunday). 'King' class 4-6-0 No.6029 *King Edward VIII* leans to the curve as it passes Hackney signal box's fine Down inner home bracket signal with the 1.20pm Penzance to Paddington. The train is made up of 15 vehicles. Through carriages from Kingswear and Paignton will have been added at Newton Abbot. *Peter W. Gray.*

passing through. First of all, in June 1911, the goods station was moved to a new site on the Moretonhampstead branch. This was followed by a new marshalling yard at Hackney which was opened in December 1911. The station and Hackney Yard were enlarged in 1913 and the next stage would have been a flying junction at Aller with a new station at Newton Abbot, but the onset of World War I stopped these proposals. Not until 1923 was the plan resurrected, and then without the flying junction at Aller. Despite this simplification, and following a period of high inflation, costs had now doubled compared with the pre-war scene.

The new station opened on 11th April 1927. There were two island platforms each 1375 ft long, and capable of holding two 8 or 9 coach trains on each of the four faces. The six running lines, three in each direction, replaced the 1861 station of three narrow platforms. Two large wooden signal boxes, East, with 206 levers (the second biggest on the GWR), and West, with 153 levers, replaced the four boxes previously needed to control the former layout. An imposing three-storey brick building on the street front replaced the former station offices. As part of the scheme, new running junctions had been installed at Aller Jn and a new signal box built there.

Holiday traffic on the GWR continued to increase in the 1930s, and with the first half of the following decade being occupied by the Second World War when the railways generally had far more traffic than they could comfortably deal with, even the much expanded accommodation at Hackney and Newton Abbot struggled to keep up with the flow of people and goods marked 'OHMS'. New goods loops between Newton Abbot and Hackney, and at Aller Junction,

were provided in 1941. Hackney Yard was again enlarged in 1940 and 1943, the goods yard and locomotive sidings also being extended in the latter year. On 20th August 1940 Newton Abbot railway facilities were bombed resulting in the deaths of 14 people with 15 more seriously injured.

After the War, the West Country holiday traffic once again resumed and the 1950s saw it at its peak. Peter Gray, that eminent railway photographer of the South West scene, who has contributed many of the pictures in this book, spent many a summer Saturday watching, recording and photographing the 1950s and early 1960s steam scene. In his weekly newspaper article '*Rail Trail*' he has written as follows:

> *'The new diesel locomotives were still three years in the future and train operation in 1955 was 100 per cent steam. With locomotive facilities being located at Newton Abbot, combined with the need to attach or detach assisting engines to or from almost all the Plymouth trains, there was always a lot going on.*
>
> *On top of this, it may not be apparent to today's observers of the many trains that glide - or roar - non stop through today's emasculated Newton Abbot station, that on a peak summer Saturday in 1955 there were only four trains in the down direction between 8.30 am and 8.30 pm that did not stop. To that figure must be added the 74 that did stop. With such a service good time-keeping was not expected, it was enough to keep the traffic moving steadily westwards.*

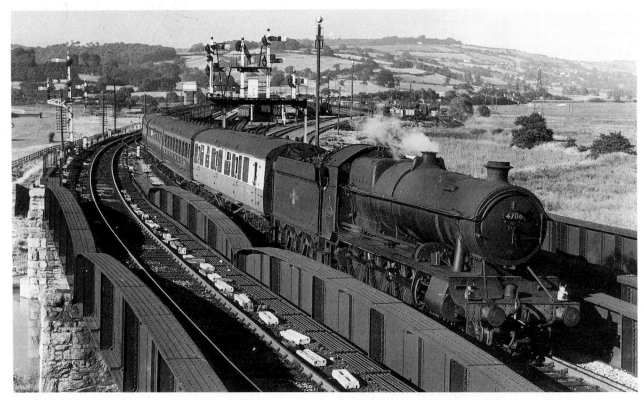

Newton Abbot, 4th July 1959. In the normal course of events, Churchward's excellent '4700' class of 2-8-0 was rarely seen in the daytime as this small class of only nine engines was almost exclusively used on express freight, milk, etc., trains which ran during the night hours. However, because of their hauling power and ability to attain a reasonable turn of speed, they were often pressed into passenger service on summer Saturdays, and the 1.25pm (SO) Paddington - Kingswear was one of their regular 'jobs'. Here No.**4706** is about to enter Newton Abbot and a fairly full Hackney Yard can be seen in the background.   *David S. Fish*

The operators at Newton Abbot really were in an impossible situation. With more and more people travelling by rail on holiday to the West Country each year through the 1950s, but with facilities which - due to the war - had barely altered since the early 1930s, they were expected to cope with a flow of trains which increased almost imperceptibly each year, always rising to a torrent on the peak Saturdays around the old early August Bank Holiday'.

On Summer Saturdays, through trains to Paignton or Kingswear often had their locomotives changed at Newton Abbot, with the fresh engine being attached to run tender first in preparation for its return working from the Torbay line to the North or London, a practice increased throughout the 1950s. This meant that station times were often exceeded and with only two down platforms available, produced a knock-on effect, the delay affecting a succession of trains approaching Newton Abbot, and on occasions as far back as Exminster. The sort of heavy delays that occurred on the peak Saturdays are well described in the book *Summer Saturdays in the West* (David & Charles), which dealt with what was probably the worst day for traffic delays ever experienced in the West of England (27th July 1957).

The problem lay in the fact that the railway was trying to cope with a tremendous peak on one day of the week, that was at its worst for only about six weeks of the year. As alternative transport became available, particularly the private car, discontented rail travellers - who were causing the congestion by their need to take holidays in those few high season weeks - started to leave the railway. At the same time a new management, under the chairmanship of Dr. Beeching, concluded that there was too much coaching stock kept for those busy few weeks, spending the rest of the year 'mothballed' in sidings - apart possibly for a few runs at Easter or Christmas - and duly scrapped them. So the 1960s saw the railway's traffic problems

steadily reducing with the 78 down trains mentioned by Peter Gray (for 23rd July 1955) between 8.30 am and 8.30 pm, being reduced to 55 for the same period on 24th July 1971. Because everything was now dieselised, no motive power changes or assisting engines were required, thus enabling station times to be cut. It is subsequently recorded in *Summer Saturdays in the West* that there were only five occasions during the whole day on 24th July 1971 when Newton Abbot's two down platforms had been occupied simultaneously, whereas - in 1957 - this was happening continually.

Since then things have changed quite dramatically. Hackney Yard closed as a marshalling yard in 1971. Newton Abbot's passenger station continued relatively unchanged until April-May 1987 when, in connection with the extension of Multiple Aspect Signalling (MAS) from Exeter, it was reduced to a three-platform operation, the former up through and up main lines being lifted and the area converted to car parking. All the signal boxes at Newton Abbot and Aller Jn were closed and Aller reverted to its pre-1925 situation of a geographical divergence point only, the physical junctions being removed and new connections put in at the west end of Newton Abbot - again as pre-1925. The timetable for the same period 8.30 am - 8.30 pm on a Summer Saturday in 1990 indicated only 47 down trains.

Newton Abbot's remaining two dozen or so railwaymen now look out over a barren waste of dirty ballast, weeds and small shrubs, and decaying buildings where once stood the busy carriage sidings, locomotive sidings, engine shed and locomotive and carriage and wagon works. It is extremely doubtful if this area will ever again be required for railway purposes, but it is a great shame that it has to be left in this state to remind everyone how things have changed and to what extent the once industrious railway centre has dropped in status. It is to be hoped that the illustrations in this book will bring back pleasant memories and help overcome this sadness.

Newton Abbot, 19th July 1958. Train No.810, the 7 am Birmingham (Snow Hill)-Plymouth enters Newton Abbot hauled by 'Castle' class 4-6-0 No.**5089** *Westminster Abbey*. It is signalled onto the Down Relief line because it carries a portion for Paignton. For the remaining 6 weeks of this summer season train 810 will be extended to Penzance.   *R.C. Riley*

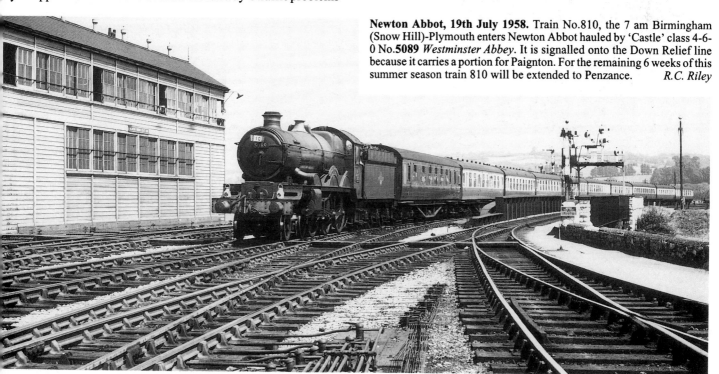

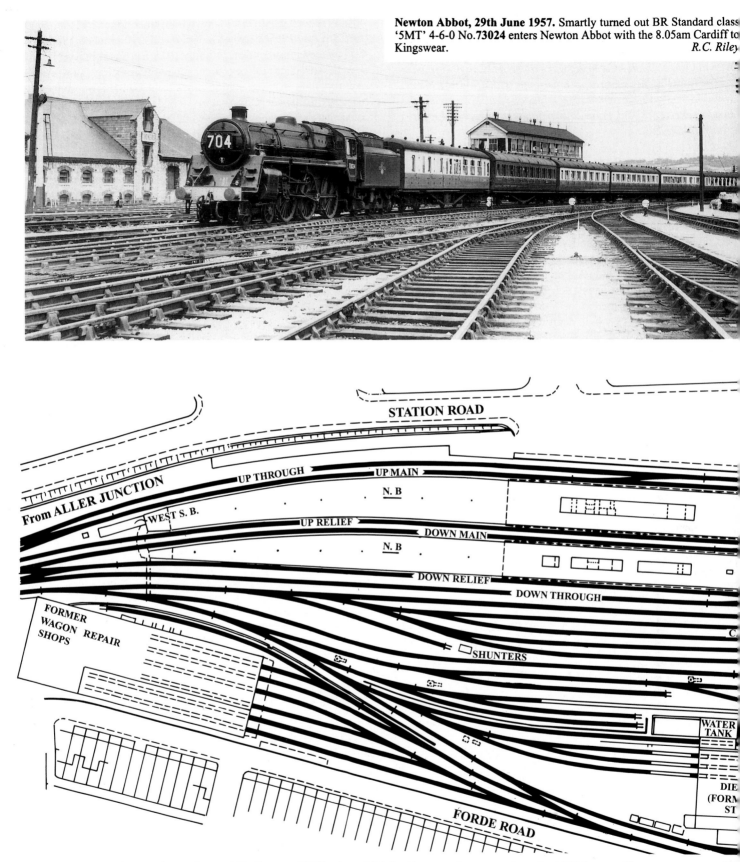

Newton Abbot, 29th June 1957. Smartly turned out BR Standard class '5MT' 4-6-0 No.73024 enters Newton Abbot with the 8.05am Cardiff to Kingswear.   *R.C. Riley*

This diagram has been redrawn from a BR (former GWR) plan which had been updated to reflect the 1972 layout. However, as was often the case with these plans, some facilities already withdrawn are still shown, such as the turntables which were removed late 1960/early 1961. This could (can) be very misleading to the historian, and such plans need to be checked against other sources before being quoted as evidence of a layout at a particular period. The six-road former steam shed had been reduced to three roads in 1972 (as shown on the plan) and in 197 the sidings in the former wagon repair shops were removed. Rail access to the former engine repair works was removed in 1978.

Newton Abbot, 29th June 1957 (Saturday). Effectively the first part of the 'Cornish Riviera Express', the 9.20 am St. Ives to Paddington pulls away from Newton Abbot Up through line, after having detached the assistant engine which has helped with the load over the Devon banks. 'King' class 4-6-0 No.**6027** *King Richard I* has steam to spare for the 3¾ hour non-stop run to Paddington.
R.C. Riley

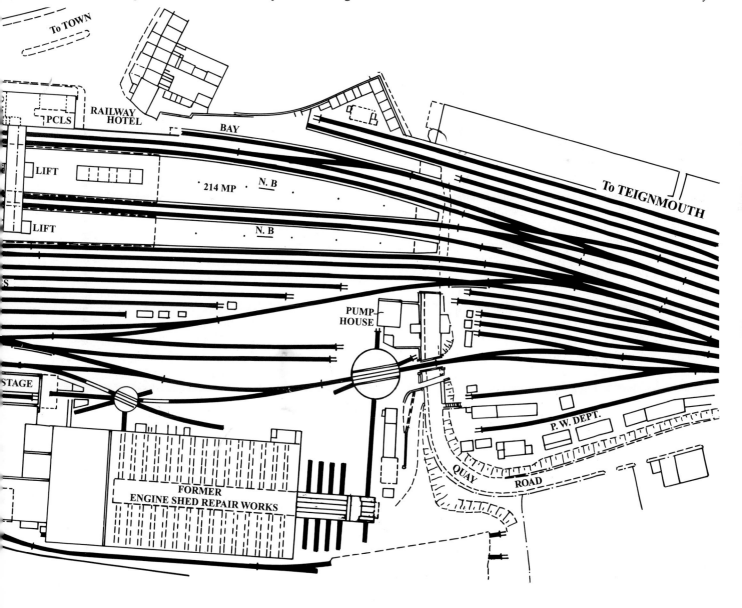

Newton Abbot, c 1957. A seldom photographed part of the layout at Newton Abbot, viewed from East box. A short, fully-fitted goods train, probably the 5.45pm from Goodrington, hauled by a tender first 'Castle' class 4-6-0 is entering the Goods Station at Newton Abbot, access to which was gained from the Moretonhampstead branch. This duty was regularly performed by the locomotive off the Down 'Torbay Express'. *David S. Fish*

Newton Abbot Summer 1958

- A glimpse at a Day's Operations

In 1958 all the branch lines feeding into Newton Abbot were still open and operating freight and passenger trains, except for the Teign Valley line from Exeter which closed to passengers on 9th June 1958. A look at the 'Saturday Excepted' (SX) pages of the Working Timetable 19th June - 14th September 1958 therefore gives an interesting insight into daily operations at this key junction before increased car ownership and Dr. Beeching removed much of the traffic. Summer Saturdays were somewhat different as practically all freight and many local trains were withdrawn to make way for the numerous extra through passenger workings, so some of the 'SX' workings will be described as more typical.

Passenger Working

Midnight to 6 am

The main business of the night was the urgent 'perishable' traffic and the 1½ hours between 2.30 am and 4 am was particularly busy.

8.20 pm	Cardiff - Plymouth Parcels	2.35	3.00
10.10 pm	Paddington - Penzance Postal	3.10	3.18
9.50 pm	Paddington - Penzance Passenger	3.29	3.36
11.0 pm	Marston Sdgs - Plymouth Fish	3.37	4.00
12.15 am	Paddington - Penzance News	3.47	3.53

Traffic for the Kingswear line emanating from these trains was despatched at 4.20 am (Torre and Paignton only), 5 am (Torre, Paignton, Churston and Kingswear) and the 5.15 am Parcels (Torre and Paignton only). Interestingly, there was a Workmen's service (not advertised) at 5.17 am to Plymouth.

During this period there were 13 down and 5 up passenger or parcels trains. All figures quoted here relate to trains that ran for at least 4 out of 5 days per week and do not include those on the Moretonhampstead branch.

6 am to 6 pm

There were 50 down and 49 up passenger or parcels trains during this period. 'Portion Working' was an interesting feature at Newton Abbot. Certain down trains would convey coaches for Penzance, Plymouth and Kingswear (or Paignton). The Kingswear line vehicles would be at the rear and would be detached by the east end carriage pilot and worked forward (by a fresh engine waiting on the down through line), usually via the scissors crossover and the down through line; departure therefore was not dependent on the clearance of the Penzance portion. In the up direction if a Kingswear portion was to be added to a train from Penzance it would run to the north end of the up main line. The engine would be detached. Several minutes later the Penzance train would arrive at the south end of the same platform. This engine would be uncoupled and would then run via the scissors crossover, to the up through line to the north end of the station and then back on to the coaches from Kingswear. Meanwhile the west end carriage pilot would have been propelling the Penzance coaches forward to join the Kingswear section. For this procedure to be completed, 8 minutes was allowed.

In the middle/early afternoon period a number of the principal express trains stopped at Newton Abbot, some of which called to pick up or set down assistant engines only:

9.30 am	Falmouth to Paddington (detach asst. engine only)	12AE53	12.55
	Up 'Cornish Riviera' (detach asst. engine only)	1AE15	1.18
12.15 pm	Kingswear - Wolverhampton	1.20	1.24
	Down 'Cornish Riviera' (attach asst. engine only)	1AE40	1.43
	Up 'Cornishman' (detach asst. engine only)	1AE49	1.52

10.5 am	Penzance - Manchester	2.05	2.10
	Down 'Cornishman'	2AE17	2.20
	(attach asst. engine only)		

In the early evening period there were no less than four trains in a single hour to get day trippers back to their holiday hotels in time for dinner, or take local workers home. They called at most stations between Paignton and Exeter:

4.40 pm	Paignton - Bristol	5.05	5.15
4.33 pm	Kingswear - Exeter	5.22	5.27
5.10 pm	Goodrington - Taunton	5.37	5.43
5.25 pm	Paignton - Taunton	5.48	5.55

6pm to Midnight

There were 23 down and 25 up passenger/parcels trains during this period. In addition on Friday nights only during the high season there was a series of Starlight Specials to North Country/Midlands destinations which called at Newton Abbot between 10.9 pm and 12.20 am (Saturday). These trains were run at special cheap fares to encourage people to avoid Saturday travel.

(Note: in the economies of 30th June 1958, 13 passenger trains serving Newton Abbot were withdrawn)

Freight Working

After midnight most activity was in the up direction with trains from Cornwall and Plymouth passing through to variously, Bristol, Cardiff, Crewe, Rogerstone, Acton, Severn Tunnel Junction and Exeter. After 6 am, however, attention focussed chiefly on the down line with the departure of goods trains to various local destinations:

6.25 am	Hackney to Kingswear
6.40 am	Hackney to Teignmouth
6.55 am	Hackney to Torre (extended to Kingswear if required)
7.0 am	Hackney to Kingsbridge
8.15 am	Hackney to Goodrington
8.55 am	Hackney to Ashburton
10.35 am	Hackney to Kingswear
11.15 am	N.A. to Moretonhampstead or Christow
11.40 am	Hackney to Ivybridge

As well as these, at very roughly hourly intervals, there were the long distance freight trains from Oxley Sidings, Severn Tunnel Jn, Reading, Bristol and Hackney itself to Plymouth and Cornwall.

Throughout the afternoon the local goods trains returned to Hackney and were marshalled into the freight trains which left each night heading north: the 7 pm Newton Abbot goods station to Acton (fast fitted, 'C' headlamps), 9.44 pm Hackney - Rogerstone (class 'F'), 11.45 pm Hackney - Avonmouth (class 'D') and 2.40 am Hackney - Rogerstone (class 'F'). Traffic for the LMR could be attached to the 1.20 am Tavistock Jn to Crewe which left Hackney at 3.40 am. Weekday freight trains which ran at least four days out of five, and including those terminating or starting at Hackney Yard, numbered 44 down and 31 up each 24 hours.

Hackney Yard

There were two pilot engines which worked continuously through the week from Monday to Friday (one started at 6 am Monday) but only one full time on Saturdays and Sundays, the other one working restricted hours on those days. A third engine worked two turns (early and late) on Mondays to Fridays only.

A further engine worked at Newton Abbot goods station from 6 am Monday to 1 pm Saturday and for a short Saturday/Sunday overnight turn.

Moretonhampstead branch

There were 8 passenger and 1 empty trains each way, plus a freight train on Mondays, Wednesdays and Fridays only. Two of the passenger trains were withdrawn from 30th June 1958.

Signal Boxes

Hackney, Newton Abbot East, West and Aller Junction were all open continuously.

Traffic Levels (1960)

BR published the following details of Newton Abbot's 1960 traffic levels:

Trains each weekday:	85 freight, 150 passenger
	(200 Summer Sats; 120 Sundays)
Passengers booked p.a.:	200,000
(and 53,000 platform tickets issued)	
Parcels forwarded p.a.:	27,000 (and 116,000 received)
Wagons dealt with at Hackney:	7,500 weekly

Newton Abbot, 19th July 1958. Train No.527, the 9.10 am Kingswear to Birmingham (Moor St) was advertised non-stop from Torquay to Swindon but actually stopped at Newton Abbot to change enginemen. It then ran via Oxford and Banbury eventually arriving in England's second city at 3.51 pm. On 19th July 1958 'Hall' class 4-6-0 No.5967 *Bickmarsh Hall* is pulling out quietly because Hackney's distant is 'on' and progress towards Birmingham may soon be interrupted. Note the fine array of double and triple disc signals in the foreground.

R.C. Riley

Newton Abbot, September 1958. The 4.25pm Plymouth (Millbay) to Paddington Parcels hauled by '4300' class 2-6-0 No.**5330** is just about to pass Newton Abbot East box. The leading vehicle is a travelling gas reservoir used to refill the gas tanks of restaurant cars.
David S. Fish

Newton Abbot, August 1957. Mixed in with, and acting as a 'relief' to, trains from further afield (although advertised in the timetable) was the 1.45pm (SO) Bristol to Newquay/Falmouth, seen here entering Newton Abbot. 'Castle' class 4-6-0 No.**5079** *Lysander* is just about to pass the magnificent East box up home signals gantry, seen before it suffered any losses through rationalisation.
David S. Fish

(top) **Newton Abbot, c 1957.** This photograph was chosen because it shows off very nicely the north end of the station - the GWR insisted on calling it the east end and this picture is taken from the East box. '9400' class 0-6-0 PT No.**9462** is quietly going about a bit of coach shunting while in the distance a short freight train hauled by a tender-first locomotive is signalled from the Up relief platform to the goods station which was located at the start of the Moretonhampstead branch, behind and to the right of the photographer. This was taken on the same day as the 'N' class locomotive and I think the short freight train is the one seen entering the Goods Station on page 14.

David S. Fish

Newton Abbot, c 1957. Southern Region class 'N' 2-6-0 No.**31837** backs into the north end of the engine shed yard at Newton Abbot **en route** to the turntable. Unfortunately the photographer has no details of what brought the locomotive to Newton Abbot, or the date. *David S. Fish*

Newton Abbot n.d., Newton Abbot shed had a bit of a reputation for not encouraging 'trainspotters' and other unofficial visitors, so on-shed photographs are rare. David Fish however obtained this fine close-up of 'Grange' No.**6836** *Estevarney Grange* and 'Castle' No.**5055** *Earl of Eldon* but did not record the date.   *David S. Fish*

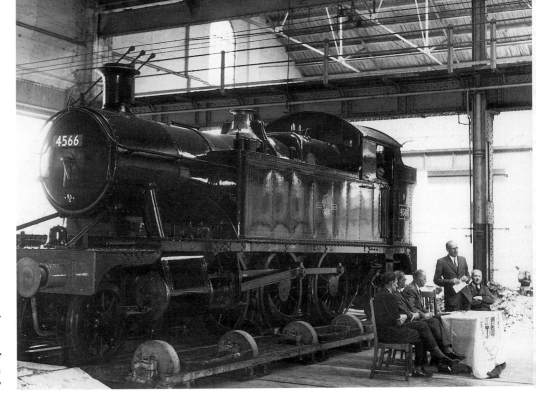

Newton Abbot, 1960. The last steam locomotive to be overhauled at Newton Abbot Locomotive Works before it closed was '4500' class 2-6-2T No.**4566**, based at Penzance. A small ceremony was held to celebrate this historic moment and the chairman of Newton Abbot Urban District Council, himself a driver, drove the engine out of the Works (15th July 1960). The locomotive was to survive following withdrawal of steam, and is now to be seen on the Severn Valley Railway. *W.L. Underhay*

Newton Abbot, MPD, 1956. Newton Abbot shed, seen 'over the wall' in 1956. '2800' class 2-8-0 No.**2875** is receiving attention from the cleaners, the only other engine which can be identified is '5101' class 2-6-2T No.**5156** behind the water crane.
David S. Fish

Newton Abbot Shed

The first locomotive shed at Newton Abbot, dating from the opening of the station, or possibly, the decision to abandon' atmospheric working', was a smallish structure 75ft x 35ft at the north end of the layout, on the Down side. By the time the GWR was contemplating the narrowing of the gauge and associated new works (1892), it must have been inadequate because £15,000 was allocated to replace it. A large new shed opened in 1893, stone built and 100ft x 150ft, accommodating six dead-end roads. There is not space here to describe the other facilities provided or the work of the adjacent locomotive factory (repair works), which deserve a separate book to themselves.

It must be remembered that at this time Ashburton, Moretonhampstead, Kingswear and Brixham each had their own locomotive shed at which the 'branch' locomotive(s) were stabled. Ashburton shed remained open until the end of that branch's passenger service (1958), Moretonhampstead until 1947, but Kingswear closed in 1924 and Brixham in 1929, Newton Abbot in turn taking over their motive power requirements.

It is interesting to compare the locomotive allocations for Newton Abbot as at May 1922 (just before the Grouping) and at 31st December 1947, the last day of the GWR's existence. Until the viaducts south of Paignton were strengthened in 1927/8, nothing heavier than a 2-6-2 tank was allowed on this section, hence the large number of locomotives of that type in 1922 (Kingswear shed had another two).

May 1922

4-6-0:	11	2-6-2T:	16	
4-4-0:	1	0-6-0T:	9	
2-6-0:	10	0-4-2T:	3	Total: 50

31st December 1947

4-6-0:	29	2-8-2T:	3	
4-4-0:	5	2-6-2T:	18	
2-8-0:	4 (WD)	0-6-0T:	7	
2-6-0:	3	0-4-2T:	4	Total: 73

Just before World War II, the GWR examined the possibility of electrifying the line between Taunton and Penzance. The cost of this would have been over £4 million. The author has an official plan showing a new 7 road locomotive shed at Aller Junction, located in the 'V' between the Torquay and Plymouth lines. Covered accommodation measured 220ft long by 156ft wide and there was provision for extension to 10 roads. The plan, dated February 1939, included a 70ft turntable and coal stage/stacking area, so it would seem that Aller would have been home to the residual steam locomotives, and that Newton Abbot would have been devoted to electric locomotive maintenance. But the electrification scheme gave an insufficient return on the investment involved and was not pursued.

Newton Abbot steam locomotive depot closed in June 1962, being supplanted by a modern diesel maintenance facility on the same site, which itself closed only 10 years later.

Newton Abbot, 3rd July 1957. In steam days Newton Abbot engines and men worked a 'double-home' express turn to Shrewsbury (Salop), alternating with Shrewsbury men. Double-home, meant lodging away from home and returning the next day with the southbound express. In this view the 'Salop' engine, No.**5097** *Sarum Castle* has arrived on shed looking almost as clean as when it started.   *R.C. Riley*

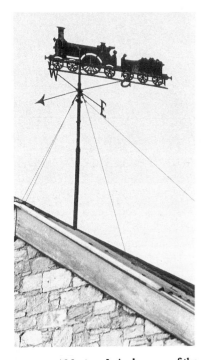

Newton Abbot. n.d. A close-up of the weather vane on Newton Abbot locomotive works. See also picture alongside.   *David S. Fish.*

Newton Abbot, 3rd July 1957. This Taunton-based 'Mogul' is fitted with automatic token exchange apparatus, used on the Barnstaple branch. '4300' class 2-6-0 No.**6364** is seen by Newton Abbot turntable. Note the Works' weathervane just above the smokebox headlamp. The building behind the locomotive was the weighhouse, used to re-balance locomotives after overhaul in the Works. Sometimes, SR engines from Exmouth Jn made use of this facility.   *R.C. Riley*

Newton Abbot. 5th March 1926. The north end of Newton Abbot station with the junction to and from Moretonhampstead line (left) in the process of being remodelled. The 1893 brick built East signal box, near the junction, is dwarfed by its all-wood replacement, a structure containing a 206 lever frame which opened on 25th April 1926. The station master at Newton Abbot had wanted four lines over the River Teign bridge, seen here just beyond the signal boxes, but the Divisional Supt. at Exeter declined to submit the proposal to the General Manager.   *British Rail.*

(below) **Newton Abbot.** On the same day as the above view, this photograph was taken from the East signal box looking towards the station. Only minimal alterations are now required to complete the remodelling connections in the middle foreground - from the Moretonhampstead line (right) to the Down Through and Middle Siding requiring installation.   *British Rail.*

Newton Abbot. June 1957. In the good old days, when there were two rail routes between Exeter and Plymouth, it was essential that train crews were able to run over the other Region's metals at short notice in the event of a mishap (flooding of the sea wall at Dawlish for example). As a precaution a Southern engine was diagrammed daily over the Western route and vice versa. On this occasion, 'Battle of Britain' class 4-6-2 No.**34057** *Biggin Hill* leaves Newton Abbot with an Up stopping service, probably the 2.15pm Plymouth to Exeter. This called at *all* stations between these places and doubtless entertained the Western stalwarts with much wheel-slipping on restarting!   *David S. Fish.*

Newton Abbot n.d., The north end of the pre-1927 Newton Abbot Station looking south. The left hand platform was used by Down line trains, the middle line by Up trains from Kingswear and the Teign Valley/Moretonhampstead branches and the right hand line was the Up main line.   *British Rail.*

Newton Abbot. 1924. The street frontage of Newton Abbot station seen in October 1924, before rebuilding started. There is an interesting collection of horse-drawn and motorised vehicles, including a motor-cycle, outside the station, even a handcart alongside the two old gentlemen on the seat (left).
British Rail.

Newton Abbot. c.1927. The imposing replacement offices provided by the GWR as part of the 1927 station. The building included the headquarters of the Divisional Locomotive Superintendent; the clock was presented to the GWR by the grateful inhabitants of the town.   *Lens of Sutton.*

Newton Abbot. In this October 1924 picture, looking towards London, rebuilding work has not yet started. The Up main line is left, the Middle line centre and the Down main line extreme right, beyond the overall roof.

British Rail

Newton Abbot. By March 1925 the centre island platform has been removed and the **new** Down main line built in its place. Note how the new Down main platform has been built out from the coping stones of the right hand platform in the upper picture.

British Rail

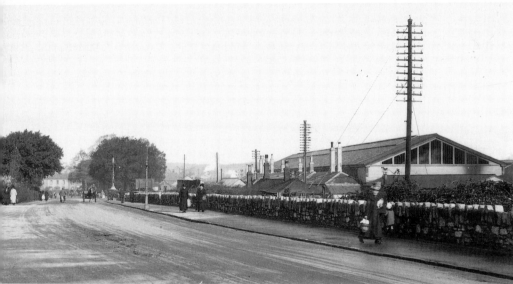

Newton Abbot. c. 1921. A view looking from south to north with Newton Abbot West box at the left of the line. This box, together with the station and its overall roof, was replaced by 1927 with the much larger new station. *LGRP*

Newton Abbot. 31st October 1923. When this photograph was taken of the Up side of the old station, looking towards London (north), the only work that had taken place was the cutting down of some trees and the removal of an embankment below the stone wall (right), prior to the building of a new retaining wall. *British Rail.*

Newton Abbot. 31st October 1923. Also looking north, this view from the Down side of the station also includes the carriage sidings and engine shed. Note the fine array of bracket signals. *British Rail.*

Newton Abbot. October 1924. In the early stages of the station reconstruction, work proceeds at the south end of the platform to the left providing ample evidence of progress in forming the new Up Through line. The extensive earthworks in the centre form the basis of the island platform that will serve the Up Main and Up Relief lines. It will be over twelve months before work begins on the main station building, the site of which is to the left of the picture.
British Rail.

Newton Abbot. August 1925. About one year into the project and remodelling at the south end begins to take shape. The siding to the left is the last of three that originally occupied the site and will ultimately be removed. The 1893-built West signal box can also be seen on the left and will eventually be replaced by an all wood structure, similar but smaller than the new East box, on 3rd April 1927. *British Rail.*

Newton Abbot, 30th December 1961. A night scene at Newton Abbot, illustrating 'Castle' class 4-6-0 No.**4037** *The South Wales Borderers*, which has run to the far end of the platform, opposite West box, in order to take water, and now awaits 'the road' westward with the 9.10am Liverpool to Plymouth.   *Peter W. Gray*

Newton Abbot, 25th April 1953. R.O.D. class 2-8-0 No.**3017** trundles past Newton Abbot West box on the up through line with a goods train. Twenty five mph was fast for these elderly locomotives, not fitted with vacuum brakes, and they also required an inordinate amount of effort from the fireman to keep the huge boiler in steam, according to the men who fired them. Note the backing signal on the post nearest the photographer. *Peter W. Gray*

Newton Abbot, c 1950. The west end of Newton Abbot station looking towards the locomotive sidings. Note the concrete post signal in the foreground.
S.J. Dickson

Newton Abbot, 25th July 1959. A classic shot of Newton Abbot as it used to be on a summer Saturday! At 4.19pm train 328, the 9.5am Swansea - Kingswear (due N.A. 2.49 - 2.55) hauled by BR Standard class '9F' No.**92234** is standing at the Down Main platform but signalled across to the Down Relief. Train 329, the 9.25am Wolverhampton - Paignton (via Swindon - due N.A. 2.58 - 3.5) is headed by 'Castle' No.**5044** *Earl of Dunraven* and will doubtless follow 328 as soon as possible. On the Down Through line, the 8.55am Wolverhampton - Penzance (due N.A. 2.27 - 2.31 for locomotive purposes only) and headed by 'Castle' No.**5021** *Whittington Castle* awaits the arrival of its pilot, No.**D6302** to assist it over the Devon banks. The carriage sidings and shed yard are a further hive of activity and three more locomotives can be seen.
David S. Fish

Newton Abbot, 25th June 1961. The 4.05pm (Sun) Paignton to Paddington approaching Newton Abbot. The locomotive is the very last 'Castle' to be built, No.**7037** *Swindon* and the leading vehicle a former GWR restaurant car. *Peter W. Gray*

Newton Abbot, 1959. Although carrying '**A**' headlamps, the Kingswear portion of the Up 'The Cornishman' called at all stations from Kingswear to Dawlish (even including Britannia Halt on Saturdays), then Exeter St. Thomas and finally St. Davids (some 1¾ hrs after leaving Kingswear), at which place it was united with the Penzance portion of the train. On a spring day in 1959 'Castle' class 4-6-0 No.**4083** *Abbotsbury Castle* coasts into Newton Abbot; on the Up main line the Up 'Cornish Riviera Express' has a clear road through Newton Abbot. *David S. Fish*

Newton Abbot, 23rd August 1955. With 2-6-2T No.**4405** at its head this is probably the Ashburton goods returning to Hackney yard. *Michael Hale*

Newton Abbot, 14th July 1955. Quite a load for a little pannier tank: '8750' class 0-6-0PT No.**3659** approaches Newton Abbot West and as it is signalled on the Up Relief line it may be anticipated to have come from the Kingswear line, the bulk of its load probably from Torre. *R.C. Riley*

Newton Abbot. 6th August 1955. A rare sight indeed in South Devon! The 8.10am Manchester to Penzance has just shed its Kingswear portion and now train engine '5100' Class 2-6-2T No.**5148**, probably fresh on at Newton Abbot, has vintage 'Dukedog' 4-4-0 No.**9023** as pilot over the S. Devon banks as it heads towards Aller Junction. Photographer Peter Gray, caught by surprise, records ' ... no time to take an exposure reading, barely time to get the camera out, unfold it, focus .... by which time the train was upon me'. However, the result is well worth including. *Peter W. Gray.*

Aller Junction. March 1954. The Down 'Cornish Riviera Express' hauled by 'King' class 4-6-0 No.**6029** *King Edward VIII* overtakes '7200' class 2-8-2T No.**7241** near Aller Junction.
David S. Fish

Aller Jn. 13th July 1957. A common racing-ground was the quadruple track section between Newton Abbot and Aller Jn. Train No.827 is the 10.35 a.m. Wolverhampton - Paignton hauled by 'Grange' class 4-6-0 No.**6807** *Birchwood Grange* and appears to be being overtaken by the more powerful combination of 'Castle' class 4-6-0 No.**4037** *The South Wales Borderers* and 'Manor' class 4-6-0 No.**7823** *Hook Norton Manor* hauling the 1.45 pm Bristol - Falmouth. It is of interest that the leading vehicle on train 827 is in Southern Region ownership.
David S. Fish

Aller Junction. 6th December 1954. 'Great Western' super-power; the first 'County', No.**1000** *County of Middlesex* pilots the first 'King' No.**6000** *King George V* on the 'Cornish Riviera Express' near Aller Junction.
David S. Fish

Aller Junction. October 1952. A nice view of Aller Junction Down home signals. Relief line - left, main line - right. The small signal arms lead to the Down goods loop.   *British Rail.*

Aller Junction. 10th August 1956. An unusual combination: 'Hall' class 4-6-0 No.**5967** *Bickmarsh Hall* and W.D. class '8F' 2-8-0 No **90179** double-head the 4.25pm Plymouth Millbay to Paddington parcels train past Aller Jn.
The late C.H.S. Owen,
courtesy Peter W. Gray

Aller Junction. The interior of Aller Junction signal box, photographed in the 1920s, possibly 1925, when it opened. *British Rail.*

Private and not for Publication.   NOTICE No. 125.

GREAT WESTERN RAILWAY.

EXETER DISTRICT.

OPENING
OF
ALLER JUNCTION.

SUNDAY, MAY 24th, 1925.

NEW SIGNAL BOX.

A New Signal Box to be named ALLER JUNCTION situated on the Down Side of the Line at 215 miles 15 chains, will be brought into use.

The Existing ALLER SIDING Box will be taken out of use and the Telegraph Apparatus transferred from it to the new Box.

NEW JUNCTIONS.

New Junctions will be brought into use as shewn on the Diagram at end of this Notice.

There will be facing Junctions from the Down Main Line or Down Relief Line to the Down Main Line or Down Branch Line and from the Up Main Line or Up Branch Line to the Up Main Line or Up Relief Line.

The Existing Lines between Newton Abbot West and Aller will, on and from this date, be as under :—

EXISTING.	FUTURE.
Down Branch.	Down Relief.
Up Branch.	Down Main.
Down Main.	Up Relief.
Up Main.	Up Main.

Aller Junction Signal Box will be switched out from 4-0 a.m. to 6-30 a.m. on Week-days, 4-0 a.m. to 7-30 a.m. on Sundays and from 11-15 p.m. Sundays to 6-30 a.m. Mondays.

The Signal Engineer will carry out the following Signal Alterations between the hours of 7-0 a.m. and 7-0 p.m. :—

NEW SIGNALS.
(For details see diagram).

Signal on Diagram.	Form.	Name.	Position.	Distance from Box. Yards
M	1 ⊏X⊐	1.—To be brought into use later.	Between Down Main and Down Relief Lines.	969
	2 ⊐	2.—Down Main Distant.		

Aller Junction. 12th August 1961. A rare visitor to the Kingswear line, BR Standard class '9F' 2-10-0 No.**92003** seen here is in charge of the 9.5am Swansea to Kingswear, passing Aller Jn on the 12th August 1961.
W.L. Underhay

Kingskerswell, 14th July 1956. Train No. 149, the 1.25pm Paddington to Kingswear is nearing the end of its journey. Seen here between Aller Jn and Kingskerswell, (Aller Jn Up home signal in the background), the train is hauled by a reasonably clean 'Hall' class 4-6-0, No.**4969** *Shrugborough Hall*. Although the route can hardly be described as "switchback" a testing two and a half mile climb at 1 in 110 will now be encountered before the short descent into Torre.   *David S. Fish*

Kingskerswell, Tuesday, 8th May 1956. Highly-polished 'Castles' Nos.**7024** *Powis Castle* and **5044** *Earl of Dunraven* are about to pass Kingskerswell with the Down empty Royal Train, 11.15am Barnstaple (Victoria Rd) to Goodrington. The Royal Train itself left Torquay that night at 11pm, for Grampound Road in Cornwall.   *David S. Fish*

The Torbay Line

This line had a most complex history for a railway of less than 15 miles in length. The first five miles to Torre was owned by the South Devon Railway and opened as early as 1848. With this the residents of Paignton, Brixham and Dartmouth had to be content until 1859 when the line was extended to Paignton by an independent company, the Dartmouth & Torbay Railway, although trains were worked by the South Devon Railway from the outset. Extended first to Brixham Road in 1861 - renamed Churston in 1868 - the Dartmouth & Torbay portion of the line eventually reached Kingswear in 1864 after total expenditure of over ¼ million pounds, against Brunel's estimate, admittedly seriously under-estimated by persuasion of the Directors, of £90,000. Even this huge figure excluded expenditure on the facilities at Kingswear. With no money coming in, the Dartmouth & Torbay Directors had formed the Dartmouth Harbour Commissioners, a body which was able to raise cash by alternative methods not involving railway Parliamentary procedures!

The cost of construction had overstretched the Dartmouth & Torbay finances and so the railway was leased to the SDR from 1st January 1866 and amalgamated with it on 1st January 1872. However, the SDR was itself leased to the GWR from 1st February 1876 and amalgamated with the Great Western on 1st August 1878.

Initially a single track route, the growing popularity of Torquay as a health resort caused a fairly regular expansion of facilities. The first section from Torquay Junction (Aller) to Kingskerswell was doubled in 1876 and on to Torquay in 1882. A new, much improved Torquay station was opened in 1878. Doubling beyond Torquay to Paignton was not carried out until 1910, and the final widening works, the short section on to Goodrington, was carried out in 1928 when a new halt was also opened. The final heavily-engineered stretch to Kingswear has always remained single line, with a crossing loop at Churston, junction for Brixham from 1868-1963. Perhaps more so than any other GWR secondary line (and possibly even any other similar line in the country), in the 20th century, until recently, the Kingswear line always enjoyed a first class service of through trains from all parts of Britain, dramatically expanded on summer Saturdays when trains literally queued up to reach Paignton. Unfortunately this station was always a bottleneck comprising only two platforms and intersected by a level crossing at each end, one of which carries the town's principal shopping street and route to the sea front. During the depression of the 1930s, the Government asked major employers to prepare schemes to alleviate unemployment. As a part of the GWR's package of proposals, a plan was put forward for a major enlargement of Paignton to include five through platforms and replacement of the south level crossing by an overbridge. The level crossing at Goodrington would similarly be replaced by an overbridge, and new carriage sidings and locomotive watering facilities, and a turntable, were to be provided nearby.

Sadly, as happened with Newton Abbot 25 years earlier, the onset of War stopped the work and Paignton never saw its marvellous new station. Eventually, the Goodrington element of the proposals was completed - as part of the 1955 Modernisation Plan. The new steam engine facilities opened as late as 1956, only nine years before steam left the Western Region for good.

Thanks to the presence of a large gasworks at Preston, midway between Torquay and Paignton, there was an appreciable amount of coal traffic on this 'Holiday Line', apart from the general merchandise conveyed to the businesses and shops of Torquay, Paignton, Brixham and Dartmouth. This coal came in by sea to Kingswear in 1,100-1,700 ton consignments and it took two days to unload this and move it in special trains for Torquay Gasworks. About 150 wooden bodied wagons were needed to clear a cargo - or some 120 of the larger capacity steel wagons. The empty wagons were assembled at Hackney Yard in three sets when the ship was due and these then shuttled backwards and forwards until the ship was cleared. During World War II this gas coal came by rail throughout to Torquay, but household coal in smaller consignments of about 600 tons continued to come to Kingswear by sea during the war, and was unloaded to rail. After 1963 the gas coal again came by rail throughout, but the gasworks closure in 1968 brought to an end this source of revenue.

In January 1972 British Rail advertised its intention to close the section of line between Paignton (exclusive) and Kingswear. However, the Dart Valley Railway, which now owned the line from Totnes to Buckfastleigh, negotiated the purchase of this section and ultimately took it over from 30th December 1972. Since then it has been worked by steam during the summer months - closing during the winter. Holidaymakers and steam enthusiasts may continue to enjoy the delights of its attractive scenery, hauled by genuine ex-GWR locomotives. Long may it continue!

Kingskerswell, 6th August 1955. On Summer Saturdays it was necessary to press into service almost everything that moved to power the heavy timetabled service of (nominally) express trains, plus extras, to and from the West Country. On any other day of the week it would be unusual to see the mixed traffic 'Grange' class hauling express trains (at least east of Plymouth) because of their relatively small driving wheels, but on Saturdays every little bit helped. So here is No.**6815** *Frilford Grange* heading the 8.6am Sheffield to Kingswear on the last stage of its journey, running into Kingskerswell. Kingskerswell lost its passenger services on 5th October 1964, being the only station on the line to do so at the time.
Peter W. Gray

Kingskerswell. c.1920. An Up stopping train has just left Kingskerswell and from the expression on the station master's face one wonders whether he is going to rebuke the photographer for some reason. The appearance of this station hardly altered over the years, apart from the lengthening of the platforms in 1911.
Peter E. Baughan collection.

Shiphay Bridge, 28th July 1951. At 9.45am on a peak Saturday morning, a trio of light engines has just passed under Shiphay Bridge north of Torre and is running gently down the bank towards that station. At the front is 'Castle' 4-6-0 No.**4099** *Kilkerran Castle*, then 'Castle' No.**5094** *Tretower Castle* and bringing up the rear 'Hall' No.**6934** *Beachamwell Hall*. The photographer later recorded the engines at Newton Abbot on Up trains as follows: 5094 on 9.00am Paignton - Manchester (load 10) at 9.49am; **6934** on 9.15am Paignton - Leeds (545 - load 8) at 9.58am and **4099** on 9.45 am Churston - Paddington (load 11) at 10.37am. The latter train catered for Brixham holidaymakers and ran non-stop from Paignton to Paddington. *Peter W. Gray*

Shiphay Bridge. 13th July 1957. Train No. 508, a relief to Paddington, approaches the Torre Up outer advanced starting signal, at 8.53am. 'Hall' class locomotives were allowed 11 vehicles unassisted up the 1 in 55 grade out of Torquay so No. **4922** *Enville Hall* should be coping without difficulty.

Peter W. Gray

Torre, 10th May 1958. '1400' class 0-4-2T No.**1427** will have to work hard, probably in full forward gear, to pull its trailing load of over 100 tons up the bank out of Torre. The train is the 10.5am Paignton to Moretonhampstead and consists of two auto-trailers, plus a cafeteria car which will be detached at Newton Abbot. Torre station provided welcome relief for Up goods trains on the stiff climb from Torquay. As the notice displays, Down trains were to take precautions against the 1 in 55 descent.
Peter W. Gray

Torre, 9th August 1958. At the other end of Torre, '4575' class 2-6-2T No.**5533** banks the 8.52 am Paignton to Sheffield under Torre's ornate footbridge; it will push as far as the outer advanced starter whence train engine No.**6997** *Bryn-Ivor Hall* will have to manage on its own. Just entering the Down platform is a train double-headed by two 4-6-0s, No.**6852** *Headbourne Grange* running tender first, and No.**5949** *Tremeton Hall.*
Peter W. Gray

Torre c 1866. Quite why this photograph was taken is a mystery. The broad gauge locomotive around which the men are grouped is the South Devon Railway 4-4-0T *Zebra*, built in October 1866. First seen in a series of 19th century reminiscences appearing in the local Torquay paper in the 1920s, the photograph was dated by that author as being 1868. When it next surfaced in the *History of Torquay* by John Ellis in the 1930s, the latter had redated it 1866 (i.e. if so, *Zebra* would have been brand new). Anyhow, the scene is Torre Station, which obviously had a sizeable staff!

Torquay Natural History Museum

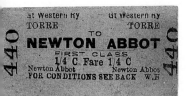

Torre, 26th April 1958. The driver of the 8.55am Newton Abbot to Kingswear local train failed to observe the Torre Down distant at caution or the two home signals at danger, and smashed into the brakevan of a short freight train standing on the Down line. As can be seen, the rearmost coal wagon, made of wood, was completely demolished and 'Castle' class 4-6-0 No.7004 *Eastnor Castle* was quite badly damaged at the front end. Train services were badly disrupted until the Up line was reopened at about 2.50pm. Public goods services were withdrawn from Torre on 4th December 1967, although the latter couple of years had only seen coal traffic.

Peter W. Gray

Torquay. 21st May 1892. On the last day of the broad gauge, an unidentified former SDR 4-4-0T locomotive leaves Torquay for Kingswear. The middle siding appears to have been converted to standard gauge already. *Torquay Natural History Museum*

Torquay. Probably photographed on the same day, a view through Torquay station, looking from south to north. Alternate transoms have been cut through in preparation for the narrowing of the gauge. *Torquay Natural History Museum*

Torquay. 19th September 1953. The empty coaches to form the 10.30am non stop train from Torquay to Paddington arrive at Torquay. This entailed the manning of the ground frame (right), the former Torquay North signal box, opened in 1878 and reduced to a ground frame in 1910, to cross the train to the Up line. (Opposite) 'Castle' Class 4-6-0 No.**4080** *Powderham Castle* runs round the same coaches at Torquay prior to working the train forward to Paddington while the fireman watches from the platform, no doubt with a can of hot water for tea-making in his hand. At the other end of the station 2-6-2T No.**5557** is going to the rear of the train ready to bank it to Torre.
(Both) Peter W. Gray

Torquay. n.d. On a wet Sunday in the 1960s single line working is in operation over the Down line between Torquay and Torre whilst relaying is taking place on the Up line. **D6330** prepares to ascend the steep incline to Torre; the ground frame immediately in front of the locomotive controlled the connections to the Up sidings and middle siding, as well as the facing crossover beyond the stone overbridge in the distance.
W.L. Underhay.

Torquay, 10th July 1958. The Up 'Torbay Express' begins the steep climb between Torquay and Torre, hauled by 'Castle' Class 4-6-0 No.**5034** *Corfe Castle.* *R.S. Carpenter collection.*

Torquay
–For sunshine

Wonderful, wonderful Torquay . . . the exciting holiday resort where it's the sunshine season *any* season!

There are hundreds of sights to see . . . places to go . . . things to do. Sparkling beaches . . . fabulous gardens—shaded walks, and a romantic wonderland of theatres, cinemas, concerts, cafes and dancing to make this your most memorable holiday, ever.

Visit Torquay, the Queen of the English Rivieras, this year . . . you'll be so glad you did!

Write for full colour guide to John Robinson,

60 Publicity Offices, Torquay (1/- P.O.)

TRAVEL BY TRAIN

Torquay. 1950. Torquay Down side building is dressed overall and the sign reads '1950 Welcome to Torquay Carnival Week'. A fine array of taxis is lined up awaiting customers.
British Rail

Torquay. 20th November 1957. Torquay Down side booking hall.
British Rail.

Torquay. November 1957. Torquay Down side booking office.

British Rail.

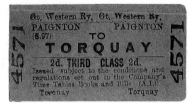

Torquay. 20th November 1957. Home comforts indeed in this view of the Down side waiting room. An almost ecclesiastical air prevails with a selection of framed pictures illustrating what appears to be cathedrals. As if to indicate that someone occasionally used the facilities, newspapers have been carefully positioned. Latterly, the small carpet would more than likely have found itself in the office of a supervisor or local manager. *British Rail.*

Torquay. July 1958. Torquay Down side garden seen in July 1958; the small sign stated that the garden was maintained by the Corporation Parks Department. The spacious house behind the hedge was owned by BR and rented by the station master. *British Rail.*

Livermead. 28th June 1952. Doubtless carrying some very tired passengers, and running almost an hour late, the 11.15pm Manchester (Victoria) to Paignton climbs the steep 1 in 56 gradient between Torquay and Paignton. The locomotive is 'Star' class 4-6-0 No.**4052** *Princess Beatrice* which was withdrawn exactly a year later in June 1953.
Peter W. Gray

Livermead. 19th May 1956. More usually employed on short branch lines, this auto-train consisting of '1400' class 0-4-2T No.**1466** propelling two trailers is the 8.40am Moretonhampstead to Paignton through service, here seen passing Gas House Sidings distant signal. This location was the site of a collision between two passenger trains on 25th August, 1962.   *Peter W. Gray*

Torquay Gasworks, 1903. Two photographs taken following a major landslip near Torquay Gasworks, between Torquay and Paignton, in the late evening of 3rd February, 1903. The cliff was undermined by the sea, leaving the track hanging. Fortunately, a watchman was employed there and stopped an approaching train in time. In the top view, looking towards Paignton, the damage is apparent; with the track having been slewed further inland. The additional tracks to the right are Gas Works sidings. The lower view is looking in the opposite direction, through Livermead tunnel towards Torquay. The section between Torquay and Paignton was doubled in 1910, at which time the tunnel was opened out.

Photo:(Both) Torquay National History Museum

Torquay Gasworks, 9th July 1961. On Summer Sundays there were several trains which started from fairly unusual places not too far distant from Torbay which were intended as 'timetabled excursions' for the local populace. This is the 9.30am Bridgwater to Goodrington which is passing Gas House Sidings behind '4300' Class 2-6-0 No.**7311**.

W.L. Underhay

Torquay Gasworks 1947. A panoramic view of the Torquay line at its closest point to the sea, at Gas House Sidings between Torquay and Paignton. The signal box, opposite the main gas works building, was normally switched out except for trains calling and on Summer Saturdays when it was opened from 6 am to 6 pm to deal with the intense holiday traffic. The gas works is still in wartime camouflage although this photograph is dated 1947, and note the pill box immediately in front of the first telegraph pole, part of the wartime coastal defences.

British Gas - South Western

Paignton, n.d. Paignton South signal box which controlled Sands Road level crossing at the Kingswear end of the station and the access to the Goodrington Carriage Sidings until its closure in 1989. The signalmen now sit in a small room adjacent to the booking office and never see a train, the barriers at Sands Road being operated by traincrew.   *British Rail*

Paignton. 16th July 1946. An unusual view of the south end of Paignton station viewed from the Up main line. Sands Road level crossing and Paignton South signal box are in the centre of the picture; possibly the level crossing gates have just been renewed. Note the locking bar in the Down line, a device used to prevent the signalman reversing points while a vehicle was standing on it. Nowadays, track circuiting is used to carry out this function.   *British Rail*

Goodrington. 16th July 1946. Goodrington Sands Halt looking south towards Churston. New carriage sidings, an engine turntable and watering facilities were provided on the waste ground behind the stabled coaches in 1956. Today that land has again become 'waste ground' - a car park!   *British Rail.*

Goodrington. 16th July 1946. Goodrington Sands Halt looking north towards Paignton. At the platform ends are bridge abutments, the building of which was intended to replace the level crossing, but work was interrupted by World War II and not completed until 1956. There is another photograph (seen in my book *The Newton Abbot to Kingswear Railway*) which shows possibly the same set of coaches stabled in the Up side siding in August 1945!

British Rail

Goodrington, n.d. The attractive all timber signal box at Goodrington. This closed in 1972, just before the section between Goodrington and Kingswear was sold to the Dart Valley Railway Co. BR retained ownership of the line between Paignton and Goodrington, over which the private company enjoys 'running powers'. *David Nicholas*

Three Beaches, 13th April 1957. 'Castle' class 4-6-0 No.**5053** *Earl Cairns* hauls the Down 'Torbay Express' past Three Beaches between Goodrington and Churston. Torquay can be seen in the background across the bay. *Peter W. Gray.*

Near Churston. 8th July 1956. The Up 'Torbay Express' (somewhat unusually without headboard) is powered by 'Castle' class 4-6-0 No.**4082** *Windsor Castle*. The train is between Churston and Goodrington on one of the two single track sections of the Kingswear line. *Philip J. Kelley*

The Brixham Branch

This little line was only two miles long but survived until the 1960s on a staple diet of fish! Opened on 28th February 1868 by the Torbay and Brixham Railway (T & B) as an independent broad gauge branch, it managed to retain its independence until 1883 when it was absorbed into the GWR. At the beginning of its existence the line was worked by the South Devon Railway, albeit it owned its own locomotive, a little 0-4-0 called *Queen*. Unfortunately, the South Devon Railway's (SDR) accountancy methods entailed payment for the fish traffic only for the two miles from Brixham to Churston at mileage rates and the T & B never paid a dividend for eight years despite carrying about 1,500 tons of fish and 70,000 passengers per year. Negotiations with the SDR during 1875 were unsuccessful and so the Torbay & Brixham decided to pull out of its working agreement with them and run its own trains. They continued to hire rolling stock from the SDR until its takeover by the GWR on 1st February 1876, after which time the GWR provided vehicles until June 1876 when the Torbay & Brixham took over the trains itself. In 1876 the Torbay & Brixham took the South Devon Railway to the Railway Commissioners, claiming that it had been unfairly treated and not received the proper allowances for provision of handling facilities at Brixham for dealing with fish traffic, which the SDR had claimed, and been paid for, as if the traffic had originated at Churston. The South Devon Railway was found to be in error and

had to pay the substantial sum of £2,135, less £350 which they had loaned to the Brixham company in 1868.

Over the next few years costs continued to rise and although fish tonnage averaged about 2,000 tons a year (compared with 800 when the line opened) and some 80,000 passengers annually were carried, dividends were paid only in two half-years in 1876 and 1877. From then onwards the balance sheet stayed in the red and capital was only raised by share issues taken up by the Directors. Approaches were made to the GWR as early as 1879 suggesting a take-over, but the little line priced itself too high and GWR would not bite. Eventually in 1882, a sale price of £12,000 was agreed (a real bargain, less than half the cost of the line's construction although the GWR inherited a deficit of £2,743).

From then on the branch became a fairly insignificant part of the GWR, although it continued to be well used by passengers until the advent of motor buses in strength, after World War I. Fish traffic remained strong until the end but eventually, a combination of the Beeching era and the need for heavy expenditure on infrastructure renewals caused it to be closed completely on and from 13th May 1963. Unfortunately, standard gauge preservation schemes were hardly thought of then and the station site at Brixham was soon built over, preventing the line ever reopening, unlike the nearby Paignton to Kingswear main line section.

Churston. 11th March 1960. A pair of Newton Abbot (83A) locomotives form the focal point of this view from the north end of Churston station. Castle Class 4-6-0 No.**5055** *Earl of Eldon* leaves with "The Cornishman", the time 12.30pm, as the Brixham branch train, with 1400 Class 0-4-2T No.**1470** in charge, awaits departure time. The "Cornishman" had a history going back to broad gauge days but the title succumbed with the emergence of the "Cornish Riviera" express. Revived in the early 1950's, the name "Cornishman" was given to a service between Wolverhampton and Kingswear/Penzance. The view here shows the Kingswear portion, depart 12.15pm, which will link up with the Penzance portion at Exeter.   *P.W. Gray.*

Churston. 7th July 1956. '1400' Class 0-4-2T No.**1472** prepares to leave Churston with the 5.48pm train for Brixham. During the week, this was the last train of the day, with a return from the branch terminus at 6.30pm. The Auto trailer vehicle is W222W. Well known pianists of the day, Rawicz and Landauer, along with comedian Harry Worth, could be seen for the summer season at Torquay, one of the many features designed to entertain holidaymakers during their annual visit. *P.J. Kelley.*

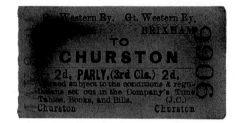

Churston. 18th February 1961. A winter service, much reduced from that during the high season, sees 0-4-2T No.**1470** set out from the bay platform with a Brixham train. *W.L. Underhay.*

Churston, n.d. A 1950s view of the north end of Churston station, with a '1400' class 0-4-2T rounding the curve towards Brixham. The single siding which comprised Churston Yard (extreme right) is at present empty. The siding to the left of the brake van is Churston Down refuge, very useful for holding empty coal wagon trains bound for Kingswear (where shipborne coal for Torquay Gasworks was loaded. Note the 'runway' trap points, left; the single line section onwards to Goodrington descended steeply from here.   *Oakwood Press*

Churston, 7th July 1956. This is how Churston used to be on Summer Saturdays in the 1950s and early 1960s! In the Down platform, almost an hour late, is the 10.20am Paddington to Kingswear hauled by No.**4082** *Windsor Castle*, with 10 very heavily loaded coaches. In the Up platform the 3.20pm Kingswear to Cardiff, headed by 'Hall' No.**4973** *Sweeney Hall*, is waiting for the imminent arrival of the signalman with the token for Goodrington. In the bay '1400' class 0-4-2T No.**1472** blows off impatiently as it awaits departure for Brixham and, alongside, stands a coach with holidaymakers for the camps on the Berry Head side of Brixham.   *Peter W. Gray*

Churston. 11th March 1960. '1400' Class 0-4-2T No.**1470** takes on water at Churston before another trip to Brixham. *Peter W. Gray.*

Churston, 25th March 1961. Three weeks after dieselisation of the branch, railcar **W55019** approaches Churston. These desirable units were produced by the Gloucester Railway Carriage and Wagon Company to seat 65 passengers. Of the twenty originally built, eight had survived into 1990 under the Class 122 identity. *W.L. Underhay*

Churston. On a Sunday in the early 1950s, Driver Reg Westaway suns himself on the footplate of '4400' class 2-6-2T No.**4406** in an idle moment during engineering work on the Brixham branch. Normally Reg only handled the '1400' class 0-4-2T on the branch passenger service, so this must have felt like a 'King' by comparison!
David S. Fish

Brixham. n.d. Holiday 'crowds' wait for a service from the small terminus at Brixham. As evidenced by the large number of empty trucks in the background, that all-year-round fish traffic was far more important than the passenger traffic which was very sparse out of the holiday period, the station being inconveniently sited high above the town. *Lens of Sutton*

Churston, June 1936. This is David Fish's first railway photograph, thought to have been taken in June 1936, and shows the streamlined 'King' class 4-6-0 No.**6014** *King Henry VII* leaving Churston with the Up 'Torbay Express'. The Brixham branch train can just be seen in the bay.

Churston, 19th May 1957. On this occasion preserved 4-4-0 No.**3440** *City of Truro* brought an excursion train from Swindon to Kingswear and is here seen heading light through Churston back to Kingswear after servicing at Newton Abbot.   *Peter W. Gray*

Greenway Tunnel, 27th August 1960. Illustrating the 'main line' status of the Kingswear line, here is Cardiff Canton's '9F' 2-10-0 No.**92216** leaving Greenway tunnel on the last couple of miles of its run with the 9.5am Swansea to Kingswear. The train is due at Kingswear at 3.50pm and is only 15 minutes late. This double chimneyed member of the class was less than twelve months old when this picture was taken. A Swindon built engine, **92216** was based at South Wales sheds throughout its short six year life, being withdrawn whilst at Severn Tunnel Junction in December 1965.

Peter W. Gray

Noss Shipyard curve, 7th August 1961. No.**6146** of the '6100' class 2-6-2T rounds Noss Shipyard curve near Kingswear, with the 3.35pm Exeter - Kingswear stopping train. This appears to be conveying eight or nine vehicles. The equivalent service today would be a 2-car dmu!

W.L. Underhay

Kingswear, 8th July 1956. Kingswear must have been one of the most attractive locations for a terminus on the GWR, even though the company was not exactly short of pleasant scenery elsewhere. In this evocative view, Waterhead Creek can be seen in the foreground, with the main line crossing it by means of Hoodown viaduct in the middle distance. In the background is the River Dart, and of course Dartmouth, with the Royal Naval College prominent on Mount Boone at the top of the picture.   *Philip J. Kelley*

Kingswear, July 1959. 'Castle' class 4-6-0 No.**5053** *Earl Cairns* passes Britannia Crossing with 'The Devonian', the 8.45am Kingswear-Bradford. The 'Floating Bridge' or Higher Ferry can be seen, just setting out for Dartmouth. *David S. Fish*

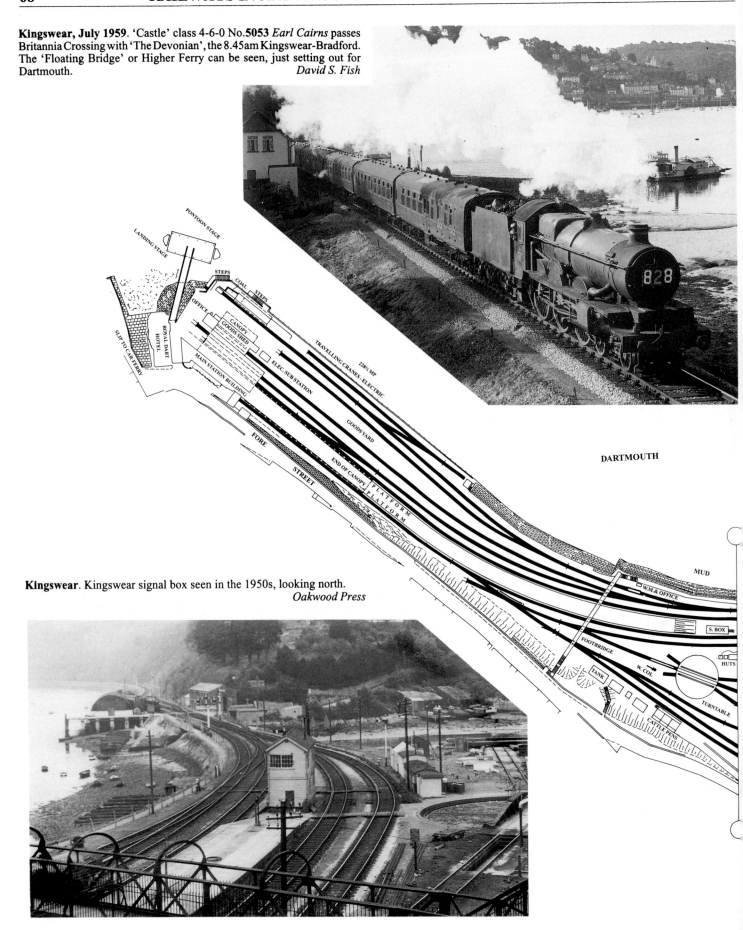

Kingswear. Kingswear signal box seen in the 1950s, looking north. *Oakwood Press*

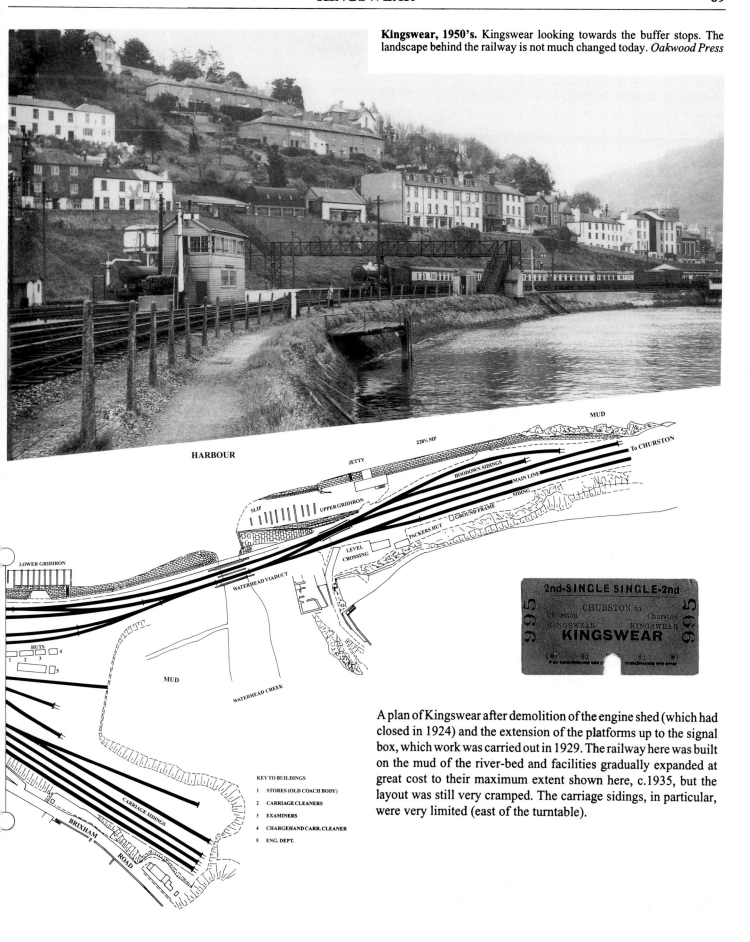

Kingswear, 1950's. Kingswear looking towards the buffer stops. The landscape behind the railway is not much changed today. *Oakwood Press*

KEY TO BUILDINGS

1 STORES (OLD COACH BODY)
2 CARRIAGE CLEANERS
3 EXAMINERS
4 CHARGEHAND CARR. CLEANER
5 ENG. DEPT.

A plan of Kingswear after demolition of the engine shed (which had closed in 1924) and the extension of the platforms up to the signal box, which work was carried out in 1929. The railway here was built on the mud of the river-bed and facilities gradually expanded at great cost to their maximum extent shown here, c.1935, but the layout was still very cramped. The carriage sidings, in particular, were very limited (east of the turntable).

Kingswear, c 1926. 'One of a series of photographs taken by the GWR about 1926 before this three span viaduct at Hoodown was rebuilt to accommodate a double track. Features of interest are the cattle pens (centre left), signal box (centre right). The engine shed can be made out with difficulty to the right of the signal box, behind the footbridge. This was closed in 1924 and demolished in 1929. *British Rail.*

Kingswear. 25th May 1955. 'Castle' class 4-6-0 No.**5053** *Earl Cairns* waits to leave Kingswear with the Up 'Torbay Express'. *Oakwood Press*

Kingswear. 24th June 1958. Viewed from the road, on which cars are queuing to join the car ferry (Lower Ferry) to Dartmouth, Kingswear station is seen here looking north. One of Everard's colliers is alongside the quay and the electric cranes are unloading coal to trucks that will be despatched to Torquay Gas Works. A train is being backed into the main platform, possibly the 'Torbay Express' coaches. *British Rail.*

Kingswear. 24th June 1958. This picture shows part of the station building at Kingswear and the Royal Dart Hotel, opened by the South Devon Railway in 1866 (as the 'Yacht Club Hotel'). Its main aim was to accommodate passengers using the mail steamers then serving Dartmouth, but after these switched to Southampton in 1891, it doubtless was more of a struggle to survive. Nevertheless, it remained in railway ownership until sold to the Dart Valley Railway in 1972. *British Rail.*

Kingswear. 24th June 1958. Kingswear goods shed (built 1866) and goods sidings; this picture demonstrates how the railway was built on the foreshore at Kingswear. Note the lifebelt on the goods office.   *British Rail.*

Kingswear. c.1925. The approach to Kingswear gangway (to the passenger ferry - left) and goods yard (right). Note the 'spur' stone to the right of the gangway to protect the foot of the building.   *Author's collection.*

Dartmouth

Although the Dartmouth & Torbay Railway Act (1857) included the town of Dartmouth in its title, the Act provided for construction from Torre to a point short of Kingswear only, at Hoodown. But provision was also made for a ferry service across to Dartmouth and the necessary piers and landing places. An attempt was made in 1860 to deviate the line to Dittisham Ferry, with a view to bridging the Dart at a later date, but this was foiled by a local landowner whose estate would have been crossed by the proposed line. In 1863 permission was obtained to extend the railway from Hoodown to Kingswear.

Failure to reach Dartmouth meant that a ferry connection was particularly important to the railway. The railway's 'Steam Ferry' (or passenger ferry) was operated on behalf of the railway by the Dartmouth Steam Packet Co. from 1864 until 1872 when the South Devon Railway took over operation itself. The boats employed were *Perseverance* from 1864 - 1869, *Dolphin* (which inherited *Perseverance's* engine and boiler) from 1869 - 1908, *The Mew* from 1908 - 1954 and the 'twins' *Adrian Gilbert* and *Humphrey Gilbert* from 1957 to 1972 when BR sold the ferry to the local council.

In addition the South Devon Railway purchased, in a sale concluded

Kingswear. 18th March 1957. Probably the best known boat on the GWR ferry service between Kingswear and Dartmouth was *The Mew* which made the short journey between the two places from 1908 until 1954. For the next 2½ years BR hired a motor launch to perform the crossing but on 18th March 1957 two new diesel engined 58ft motor vessels were brought into service by BR. These were named *Adrian Gilbert* and *Humphrey Gilbert* and *Humphrey* is seen here on that date immediately after the naming ceremony. These two vessels plied to and fro under BR ownership until the service was sold to Dartmouth Council in 1972, continuing on station until 1976 when a private operator bought the ferry service and they were replaced. *Adrian Gilbert* was returned to the service by this operator in 1978 and *Humphrey Gilbert,* by then renamed *Edgcumbe Belle* returned in 1985 after service on the Drakes' Island ferry and the Cawsands ferry.
British Rail.

3a. DARTMOUTH to KINGSWEAR (Devonshire), The "Mew."—*Address*: British Railways, Kingswear. Phone: Kingswear 203. Telegraphic Address: Stationmaster. (Map 3 **20/8** 5.)
Charges (driver and passengers included).—M/C, S. 8d.; R. 1s. Comb., . 1s. 4d.; R. 2s. Car, S. 2s. to 3s. 4d.; R. 2s. 8d. to 4s. 4d. Motor and trailer caravans not carried. Return available for one month.
Sailings from Dartmouth.—Weekdays: frequent sailings from 6.45 a.m. until 10.27 p.m. Sundays: 9.15 a.m. to 1.10 p.m.; 2.35 p.m. to 9.50 p.m. Kingswear times about ¼-hour later.

Dartmouth. 22nd January 1954. The pontoon on the Dartmouth side of the river; Kingswear station is just visible opposite. *British Rail.*

in 1873, the Kingswear Ferry (otherwise known as 'Lower Ferry' or 'Horse Ferry'), a vehicle-carrying ferry which crossed the Dart from a slip leading out of The Square at Kingswear to Bayards Cove, Dartmouth. This was originally capable of carrying one horse and cart at a time, hence its name. Unlike the passenger ferry, the railway leased this ferry out, its best known lessees being the Messrs. Casey from 1877 - 1909, later Casey & Heal, 1909 - 1925. The only regular

use the GWR made of this ferry themselves was for the conveyance of their parcels delivery vehicles to and from Dartmouth, or for consignments of animals. In 1924/5 they strengthened the landing pontoons on each side and modified the passenger ferry, *The Mew*, to allow it to carry their own road vehicles. Soon after this (in 1925) the GWR sold their vehicle ferry rights to Dartmouth Corporation.

GREAT WESTERN RAILWAY
FERRY TICKET.
DARTMOUTH
TO   (A)
KINGSWEAR
FARE 1d. C
FOR CONDITIONS SEE BACK

Dartmouth. 7th July 1954. Dartmouth station, dressed overall for Dartmouth Carnival. This station was famous as a station with no trains. There is a fine display of posters beneath the canopy. This building, now just over 100 years old, is these days used as a cafe.
British Rail

Dartmouth. c.1925. After the GWR sold their vehicle-carrying Kingswear Ferry (or 'Horse Ferry') to Dartmouth Corporation in October 1925, there was a gap in operation of the horse boats before the Corporation could find new lessees. During this period animals had to cross by the 'Steam Ferry' (the GWR's passenger ferry) much to the disgust of the public. Here, c.1925, a flock of sheep is occupying the gangway down to the pontoon at Dartmouth. There is already a lorry on the deck of *The Mew*, so there will not be much room for passengers this trip!
Author's collection.

Aller Junction. 15th October 1960. Probably destined for an engineering occupation somewhere, this unusual consignment of two breakdown cranes has just left Aller on the Down line, hauled by 'Hall' class 4-6-0 No.**4934** *Hindlip Hall* and banked by '5101' class 2-6-2T No.**5183**. *Peter W. Gray*

Aller Junction. 'County' class 4-6-0 No.**1021** *County of Montgomery* gets into her stride as she leaves Aller Jn Down loop and commences to climb the east side of Dainton bank. Doubtless there is a banker on the rear of this Plymouth bound freight. *W.L.Underhay*

Dainton Bank. 11th July 1958. Superpower for a milk train! 'Castle' class 4-6-0 No.**4098** *Kidwelly Castle* leads '2800' class 2-8-0 No.**2881** on the 12.20pm Penzance to Kensington milk train descending between Stoneycombe and Aller Junction. *Peter W. Gray*

Stoneycombe, 4th July 1958. Rear end assistance is probably very necessary here as '8750' class 0-6-0T No.**3629** heaves its short local goods past Stoneycombe's Down distant, assisted by '5101' class 2-6-2T No.**5154**.
Peter W. Gray

Dainton, 2nd May 1953. With such a toy load as this, '4500' class 2-6-2T No.**4547** needs no banker. The Ivybridge goods has just passed Dainton's Down outer distant on its journey westwards. *Peter W. Gray*

Dainton, 1954. A Down train composed mainly of loaded coal wagons is captured between Dainton's outer distant signal and the tunnel mouth, headed by '2884' class 2-8-0 No.**3866**, and assisted in rear by a banker. Dainton's Up advanced starting signal is just opposite the engine cab (although obscured by steam) and the distant signal of the box in advance (Stoneycombe) is just beyond the brake van. *R.S. Carpenter Collection*

Dainton, February 1956. When steam reigned supreme, 'King' class 4 6-0 No.**6000** *King George* V approaches Dainton summit with the Down 'Cornish Riviera'. Despite the severity of the gradient, note that the engine is 'blowing off'.   *David S. Fish*

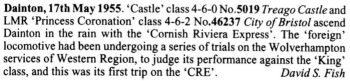

Dainton, 17th May 1955. 'Castle' class 4-6-0 No.**5019** *Treago Castle* and LMR 'Princess Coronation' class 4-6-2 No.**46237** *City of Bristol* ascend Dainton in the rain with the 'Cornish Riviera Express'. The 'foreign' locomotive had been undergoing a series of trials on the Wolverhampton services of Western Region, to judge its performance against the 'King' class, and this was its first trip on the 'CRE'.   *David S. Fish*

Dainton, 9th February 1952. The 'North Mail', 6.25am Bristol to Plymouth, nears Dainton summit, hauled by almost new 'Britannia' class 4-6-2 No.**70022** *Tornado*, a BR standard design introduced in 1951. *Tornado* was Newton Abbot's only 'Britannia' and not very well liked!
Peter W. Gray

Dainton, 6th February 1956. During 1956 there was a problem with the bogies of the 'King' class locomotives and it was necessary to draft in locomotives from other Regions to overcome the temporary shortage of the most powerful engines. On this occasion, the Down 'Cornish Riviera Express' climbs Dainton bank headed by 'Princess Coronation' class 4-6-2 No.**46257** *City of Salford*, normally based at Camden. *David S. Fish*

Dainton, 29th October 1955. On a fine autumn morning 'King' class 4-6-0 No.**6008** *King James II* nears Dainton summit with the 5.30am Paddington to Penzance (via Bristol). This train ran for many, many years and was intended as much for parcels and mails as it was for passengers - note the two parcels vans at the rear of the train.
Peter W. Gray

Dainton, 30th April 1955. The 'Austerity' class 2-8-0 locomotive was designed by Robert Riddles for the Ministry of Supply and introduced in large numbers during the War from 1943 onwards. Here, No.**90563** is just passing Dainton's inner distant with a class '**H**' freight train. Because of the severe gradient and therefore slow speed at this point, the outer distant is only a train length away and is just visible through the steam of the banker, 2-6-2T No.**4179**. Just beyond is the Up distant for Stoneycombe, 'off' as usual, because that box was only switched in occasionally for trains calling at the Quarry to load ballast, or when explosives were being used to blast away the limestone. *Peter W. Gray*

Dainton, 1930's. A North of England to Penzance express climbs Dainton bank at an unknown date, probably in the 1930s. The fireman of the leading engine, 'Bulldog' class 4-4-0 No.**3375** *Sir Watkin Wynn,* has forgotten to change his 'light engine' headcode to that of an express, which is however carried by the trailing locomotive No.**4094** *Dynevor Castle.*
The late H.J. Ashman,
courtesy I.H. Smart

Dainton, 22nd July 1959. Modern British Railways-built class '9F' 2-10-0 No.**92209** is at the head of an Up class 'C' express freight (the fastest class of freight train). Having just blasted its way up the western side of Dainton bank, the train has now breasted the summit and the locomotive has shut off steam for the descent to Aller Junction. Note that Dainton's Down inner distant is now just outside the tunnel (compare with 1955 photograph). *Peter W. Gray*

Dainton, 1921. Dainton tunnel west portal and its signal box. The sidings on either side were latterly used for the banking engines, or for the odd wagon in trouble to be detached, but had previously served the adjacent quarry.
LGRP

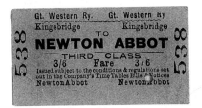

Dainton, n.d. A view of the replacement signal box at Dainton. Built in 1965 it succumbed to the march of progress in 1987, when colour light signalling controlled from Exeter replaced it.
David Nicholas

Dainton, n.d. '4300' class 2-6-0 No.**6301** emerges from Dainton tunnel with a freight bound for Plymouth and its own home depot, Laira.
W.L.Underhay

Dainton, 31st July 1959. An unusual view of the western portal of Dainton tunnel with a class 'E' Down freight hauled by 'Grange' class 4-6-0 No.**6814** *Enborne Grange.* The little signal box was replaced by a modern all timber structure in 1965. *Peter W. Gray*

Dainton 22nd April 1961. ''Warship' diesel hydraulic No.**D846** *Steadfast* roars past Dainton box on the final stage of the climb from Totnes with the 1.20pm Penzance - Paddington. The mirror above the locomotive enabled the signalman to see the tail lamp of an Up train should a Down train obstruct his normal view. Down freight trains stood here to pin down wagon brakes for the descent to Totnes. *W.L.Underhay*

Dainton, n.d. One of the 'D600' series 'Warship' class locomotives, that preceded the main 'D800' series, No.**D603** *Conquest* heads the Down 'Cornish Riviera Express' on the falling gradient towards Totnes. Because of sharp curves a speed restriction of 40 mph applied almost until Totnes was reached; the speed-limiting sign can be seen in the previous picture.

W.L.Underhay

Dainton, March 1958. In early diesel days, the Down 'Cornish Riviera Express' winds round one of the many curves between Dainton tunnel (seen in the background) and Totnes. In March 1958 the first 'Warship' No.**D600** *Active* heads for its next stop at Plymouth.

David S. Fish.

Staverton, 11th October 1958. A typical GW country branch line station? Single platform, tiny signal box, gated level crossing, all contribute to a feeling of sadness for scenes lost, although in this particular case the station and line are still open, in private hands. On 11th October 1958, just a couple of weeks before BR closed the line to passengers, the 12.15pm from Ashburton leaves Staverton en route to Totnes.

Peter W. Gray

Staverton. c.1957. This view towards Totnes shows the arrangement of the small goods yard that existed. The clerestory roofed vehicle in the distance suggests that engineering work was ongoing in the vicinity at the time, a pile of sleepers on the platform end indicating permanent way maintenance. The small "dock" to the left could perhaps hold two vehicles at the most because of the close proximity of the level crossing. *J.H. Moss.*

Between Totnes and Staverton, 6th April 1957. This must be better than bus travel! On a grey early spring day '1400' 0-4-2T No.**1470** propels the 4.55pm auto-train from Totnes to Ashburton towards Staverton along the banks of a quietly reflective River Dart.
Peter W. Gray

Buckfastleigh. The passenger facilities at Buckfastleigh. From left to right: Station Master's office; parcels office; booking office; general waiting room (through entrance doors); ladies waiting room (beyond fence).   *J.H. Moss.*

Buckfastleigh. Buckfastleigh station, seen looking towards Totnes. The passenger and parcels facilities are behind the commodious goods shed which is the prominent feature in the photograph. The line on the left of the platform line is a goods loop and two passenger trains were not allowed to cross at Buckfastleigh, but a passenger train could cross a goods train. *J.H. Moss.*

Buckfastleigh. The north end of Buckfastleigh looking towards Ashburton. The goods loop (extreme right) was signalled for both Up and Down trains. To the left of the main line can be seen the four sidings which comprised the goods facilities here; the one nearest the main line leads to the goods shed. *J.H. Moss.*

Buckfastleigh. A drivers-eye view of Buckfastleigh from the north, looking towards Totnes. Note the very short Up home bracket signal (right foreground). Wagons occupy the siding extension of the goods loop (centre left) and the headshunt to the goods yard (centre right). The signal box can be seen immediately in front of the goods shed. *J.H. Moss.*

Near Buckfastleigh, 17th July 1956. The 12.18pm from Totnes to Ashburton crosses Nursery Pool Bridge near Buckfastleigh, hauled by No.**1470**. *R.C. Riley*

Near Ashburton, 27th September 1958. Running through some of the best of Devon's scenery, the 2 pm from Totnes, comprising 0-4-2T No.1470 and a brake composite vehicle approaches Ashburton. Unfortunately the section of the branch north of Buckfastleigh was required for road improvements and does not now form part of the preserved Dart Valley Railway.

Peter W. Gray

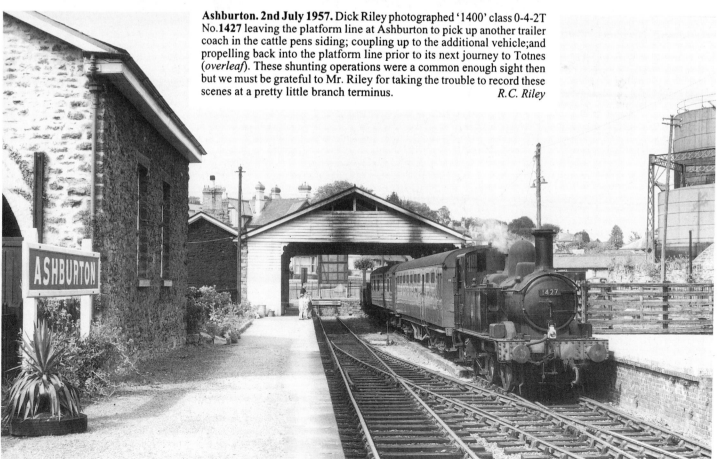

Ashburton. 2nd July 1957. Dick Riley photographed '1400' class 0-4-2T No.**1427** leaving the platform line at Ashburton to pick up another trailer coach in the cattle pens siding; coupling up to the additional vehicle;and propelling back into the platform line prior to its next journey to Totnes (*overleaf*). These shunting operations were a common enough sight then but we must be grateful to Mr. Riley for taking the trouble to record these scenes at a pretty little branch terminus. *R.C. Riley*

Ashburton. 17th July 1956. One of Newton Abbot shed's long-standing inhabitants 0-4-2T No.**1470** stands with a short freight train at Ashburton, waiting the 'road' for its return journey to Totnes, and eventually, Hackney Yard.

R.C. Riley

Totnes. c.1913. The west end of Totnes station looking towards Newton Abbot, probably about 1913. The small goods yard is full of traffic, although the platforms are deserted. The stone building prominent on the left is the former atmospheric railway engine house, never used as such owing to the abandonment of that system before it reached Totnes. *LGRP*.

Totnes. A Down express enters Totnes c.1937 hauled by a 'Star' class locomotive. The leading vehicle is one of those built in 1935 to celebrate the Centenary of the GWR. The Newton Abbot 'Target 3' duty locomotive employed on assisting trains on either Rattery or Dainton banks shares the goods shed while awaiting its next duty.   *R.S. Carpenter Collection*

Totnes. A pair of 4-6-0s double-head an Up express through Totnes, c.1927.   *R.S. Carpenter Collection*

Totnes. 17th April 1958. The Ashburton branch locomotive, Newton Abbot based '1400' class 0-4-2T No.**1427** takes water in the Up platform at Totnes. The large building opposite is the goods shed.
R.S. Carpenter Collection

Totnes. The signal box, photographed before closure which occurred in November 1987 when control was transferred to Exeter. The attractive footbridge was unfortunately severely damaged by a BR crane during an engineering occupation in October 1987, and subsequently replaced by a plain modern structure. The bridge would have been 100 years old in 1988.   *David Nicholas.*

Totnes. 15th July 1958. A Down class 'H' freight hauled by '2800' class 2-8-0 No.**2843** draws up to the water column at Totnes, prior to tackling the rigours of Rattery bank. A banker, 2-6-2T No.**5164**, waits in the Down platform and will shortly be signalled to the rear of the train to provide assistance.Note the milk tanks on either side of the station;the creamery was (and is) at the far end of the Up platform. *R.C. Riley*.

Totnes, 15th July 1958. With a good head of steam No.**2843** now blasts its way out of Totnes and up the start of the long climb to Rattery, assisted by No.**5164**. The tall chimney of the creamery (the former South Devon Railway atmospheric engine house - never used as such) can be seen protruding above the skyline. *R.C. Riley*

Totnes, n.d. This rather unusual view shows the signals at the west end of Totnes station, at an unknown date. The gantry in the foreground is about to be replaced by the bracket signal behind the small water tank; note that the signal arms are covered by an 'X' meaning 'signal not in use'. The siding on the left terminated in a small 2-road engine shed until 1904. *LGRP.*

July 1884

BUCKFASTLEIGH AND ASHBURTON BRANCH.

UP TRAINS.

Distance	STATIONS	1 Passenger arr	1 Passenger dep	2 Passenger arr	2 Passenger dep	3 Mixed arr	3 Mixed dep	4 Passenger arr	4 Passenger dep	5 Passenger arr	5 Passenger dep	6 Empty Engine arr	6 Empty Engine dep	7 Passenger arr	7 Passenger dep	SUN 1 Passenger arr	SUN 1 Passenger dep	SUN 2 Passenger arr	SUN 2 Passenger dep
...	Totnes	...	a.m. 8 40	...	10 29	...	p.m. 1 20	...	5 40	...	p.m. 5 40	...	...	...	p.m. 9 15	...	a.m. 8 5	...	p.m. 9 15
3½	Staverton	8 48	8 50	...	10 30	1 30	1 40	3 48	3 50	5 48	5 50	...	p.m.	9 23	9 25	8 13	8 15	9 23	9 25
7	Buckfastleigh	8 58	9 0	10 38	10 40	1 50	2 0	3 58	4 0	5 58	6 0	...	6 35	9 33	9 35	8 23	8 25	9 33	9 35
9½	Ashburton	9 8	...	10 48	...	2 10	...	4 8	...	6 8	...	6 42	...	9 43	...	8 33	...	9 43	...

DOWN TRAINS.

Distance	STATIONS	1 Passenger arr	1 Passenger dep	2 Passenger arr	2 Passenger dep	3 Mixed arr	3 Mixed dep	4 Passenger arr	4 Passenger dep	5 Passenger arr	5 Passenger dep	6 Empty Engine arr	6 Empty Engine dep	7 Passenger arr	7 Passenger dep	SUN 1 Passenger arr	SUN 1 Passenger dep	SUN 2 Passenger arr	SUN 2 Passenger dep
...	Ashburton	...	a.m. 7 10	...	a.m. 9 20	...	a.m 11 20	...	p.m. 2 47	...	p.m. 4 15	...	p.m. 6 10	...	7 18	...	a.m. 7 15	...	p.m. 7 30
2½	Buckfastleigh	7 16	7 18	9 26	9 28	11 30	12 0	2 53	2 55	4 21	4 23	6 17	...	7 24	7 26	7 21	7 23	7 36	7 37
6	Staverton	7 26	7 28	9 36	9 38	12 10	12 20	3 3	3 5	4 31	4 33	...	...	7 34	7 36	7 31	7 33	7 45	7 46
9½	Totnes	7 38	...	9 48	...	12 30	...	3 15	...	4 43	...	...	...	7 46	...	7 43	...	7 55	...

The Moretonhampstead Branch

Built by the independent Moretonhampstead and S. Devon Railway and opened on 26th June 1866, the Moretonhampstead branch was, like all the other lines mentioned in this book, worked by the South Devon Railway.

Just over 12 miles long, the branch served three intermediate stations initially at Teigngrace (opened December 1867), Bovey Tracey - where were situated the Bovey Potteries which employed several hundred people - and Lustleigh. The line rose in relatively easy stages between Newton and Lustleigh which was about 250ft above sea level, but in the final 3½ miles to Moretonhampstead much sharper gradients were experienced until the terminus was reached, some 500ft above sea level. The line was, of course, built to broad gauge.

Unlike the Plymouth, Torbay or Brixham lines, passenger traffic never did really develop on this branch and the passenger service was always somewhat sparse. A new station opened at Chudleigh Road (later Heathfield) in 1874, and on 9th October 1882 the station became more important when the first 6½ miles of the Teign Valley branch, to Ashton, opened to traffic. However this line was built to the 'narrow' gauge so a change of trains was necessary at Chudleigh Road.

Meanwhile the Moretonhampstead company had been amalgamated with the South Devon Railway on 1st July 1872 and became part of the GWR in 1878 when the SDR itself was absorbed. Together with the other broad gauge lines in the West Country, the Moretonhampstead branch was 'narrowed' during the weekend of 20th - 22nd May 1892, but for the moment only a siding connection joined the two lines at Heathfield and through running between these was still not possible. In 1903 the Teign Valley line was at last extended to Exeter and in 1916 a proper direct connection was installed between the two lines at Heathfield, enabling through running to take place.

In 1929 the GWR bought Lord Hambledon's country house near Moretonhampstead and turned it into the Manor House Hotel, creating a new flow of traffic for the branch. Featuring in many an advertisement in the GWR's *Holiday Haunts* brochure, the Hotel remained in railway ownership until quite recently.

Although the passenger service was withdrawn as early as 2nd March 1959, freight continued throughout the line for some years longer. However, the section from Bovey to Moretonhampstead closed completely in April 1964 and Bovey itself closed in 1967, after which Heathfield became the line's northern terminus. This 4½ mile section still remains in regular use, mainly as a result of the clay produced there, long the backbone of the line's freight traffic. In addition, an oil terminal, established in 1965, is still open.

Newton Abbot. 7th June 1958. The 5.58pm from Exeter via the Teign Valley and Heathfield has just arrived at Newton Abbot (No.9 bay platform). The motive power is '4575' Class 2-6-2T No.**5533**, a Newton Abbot engine. *Peter W. Gray.*

Newton Abbot, 18th July 1956. Ready to leave Newton Abbot for Moretonhampstead is 0-4-2T No.**1466**. Readers will be pleased to know that the engine survived to enjoy retirement at Didcot Railway Centre.

R.C. Riley

Teignbridge, 19th October 1957. The 12.45 pm Exeter-Newton Abbot via Teign Valley/Heathfield hurries past Teignbridge Crossing box on 19th October, 1957 with '8750' class 0-6-0PT No. 3677 in charge.

Peter W. Gray

Teigngrace Halt, 21st February 1959. The guard of the 5.10 pm Moretonhampstead to Newton Abbot railmotor has just left a lighted lamp at Teigngrace Halt which will be the sole means of illumination for the remaining three hours of the day's service. *Peter W. Gray*

Brimley Halt. 27th February 1959. The returning Moretonhampstead goods runs through an attractive tree-lined area between Brimley Halt and Heathfield. *Peter W. Gray*

Heathfield. 7th July 1956. A busy scene but at the same time there are not many passengers to be seen! The crew of BR Standard Class 3MT 2-6-2T No.**82001** (built at Swindon) enjoy a brief rest before leaving Heathfield, with the 10.15am Moretonhampstead to Newton Abbot. At the other end of the station '1400' Class 0-4-2T No.**1427** is ready to leave with the 10.32am Newton Abbot to Moretonhampstead, and in the bay, '5400' Class 0-6-0PT No.**5412** stands quietly with the 10.50am Teign Valley auto to Exeter.

Peter W. Gray.

Heathfield, 7th June 1958. The last day of operations on the Teign Valley line between Exeter and Heathfield sees '4575' class 2-6-2T No.**5536** on the 4.35pm from Exeter arriving in the bay at Heathfield, while the 5.10pm Moretonhampstead to Newton Abbot, being propelled by 0-4-2T No.**1427**, waits to take connecting passengers on to Newton.   *Peter W. Gray*

Bovey. 19th February 1959. Just a few days before closure to passengers, 2-6-2T No.**4150** leaves Bovey for Newton Abbot with the 10.15am from Moretonhampstead. Thirty five minutes were allowed for the 12½ miles journey, with eight trains per day in each direction. *Peter W. Gray.*

(above) **Bovey.** The schoolboy on the Up platform will not be travelling to school by train anymore for this is the last day of passenger operation as he waits at Bovey for the 7.50am from Moretonhampstead to arrive (as does the station master at the platform end). On the Down side the 7.50am from Newton Abbot runs in hauled by 0-4-2T No.**1466**. *Peter W. Gray.*

Bovey. 26th February 1959. Token exchange at Bovey with the 9.20am Newton Abbot to Moretonhampstead. The locomotive is '5101' Class 2-6-2T No.**5183.** *Peter W. Gray*

Bovey. 28th February 1959. The last day of passenger service on the Moretonhampstead branch. With suitably strengthened train and more powerful locomotive than usual, the 4.25pm Newton Abbot to Moretonhampstead leaves Bovey hauled by '5101' Class 2-6-2T No.**4117**. *Peter W. Gray.*

Bovey. 19th February 1959. The 1.35pm Moretonhampstead to Newton Abbot makes a spirited start from Bovey propelled by 0-4-2T No.**1466**. The driver is in the leading compartment of the auto-coach and he is working the regulator on the locomotive by the large lever in the coach which is connected to it. On the Brixham branch this was very rarely connected and all the driving was done from the locomotive, the driver merely acting as 'lookout' in the coach. The gong above the driver's window was used by the driver in lieu of the engine whistle when propelling. *Peter W. Gray.*

Pullabrook Halt. 21st February 1959. This illustrates wonderfully just how little the railway disturbed the tranquil countryside, unlike the roads and motorways that displaced it. The 12.50pm Newton Abbot to Moretonhampstead is formed of just a single coach, hauled by 0-4-2T No.**1466**, Pullabrook Halt being in the little cutting about 200 yards behind the train.
Peter W. Gray.

Pullabrook Halt. 3rd January 1959. The 3.15pm from Moretonhampstead to Newton Abbot leaves Pullabrook Halt with 0-4-2T No.**1466** propelling its one coach train.
Peter W. Gray.

Moretonhampstead. (upper). The exterior of Moretonhampstead station. The vintage Ford car is also interesting. (centre). Looking from Moretonhampstead station towards Newton Abbot, signal box and former engine shed to the right. (lower). The tiny signal box at Moretonhampstead was built on to one of the exterior walls of the engine shed. *all: S.J. Dickson.*

Moretonhampstead. 19th February 1959. After arrival with the 12.50pm from Newton Abbot at Moreton-hampstead, the traincrew pose for a photograph. After only a nine minute turn-round the auto-train will return to Newton at 1.35pm and the platform starting signal is already lowered.
Peter W. Gray.

Moretonhampstead. 28th February 1959. The station blackboard says it all - 'R.I.P. 1866 - 1959. A Special Train will leave Moretonhampstead 9.15pm on February 28th 1959' This photograph was taken just six hours before the sad end.   *Peter W. Gray.*